TELEGRAM FR

WILL CRIBB

Published by

INKSTAND PRESS

TELEGRAM FROM MANDALAY

An Inkstand Press book
First published in Great Britain in 2015
Copyright © William Cribb 2015
All rights reserved.

INKSTAND PRESS
Lytham St Annes, UK
www.abhaha.com

Cover design by Deeper Blue www.wearedeeper.blue
ISBN: 978-0-9572248-2-7

To Joan, who changed all our lives

2285

4

INDIAN POSTS AND TELEGRAPHS DEPARTMENT

Charges to pay.
Rs.   As.

KALIMPONG
9 OCT 30

Handed in at (Office of Origin) Mandalay C.L.

Service Instructions.

16 Words.

Recd. here at 10 H. 30 M.

TO Secretary Andrews Homes Kalimpong

Crebb arriving Calcutta october
eleventh writing

Supdt methodist mission =

CONTENTS

1

THE AVENUE

It was mid May in 2011 after attending a funeral of a former neighbour that I returned to the avenue in Oldham I had left 11 years earlier, when I was 73 years old.

I walked slowly down the gentle slope of that tree-lined avenue of modest semis — even numbers on my right, past my old dwelling on the left. I crossed the only other avenue that bisected it at right angles about halfway along its length, then looked down the steep grassy descent on the right, known locally as 'Clogger Hill'.

After all these years I wanted to see if a particular sign that I remembered was still there. Descending the path down to Mill Brow, I turned right then walked for several yards to where it joined Street Bridge Road. I turned left up Cragg Road then walked towards the spot where the River Irk ran unseen beneath my feet. The sign had shown a single finger pointing to the right, and read "KLUNDY". On the other side of the finger, pointing in the same direction, it read "T'OTHER SIDE OF KLUNDY".

The signpost was no longer there. There was no visible indication that it had ever existed. The sign had been created to professional standards, so whoever had erected it must have done so carefully and lovingly without regard to cost. I wished, like so many 'did-not-do things', that I had photographed it on one of my numerous walks up Cragg Road. Now it was too late.

But it was not too late to wonder why I was so keen to see it again. Seeing it for the first time had brought a smile to my face; I'd appreciated the wry humour, but time had allowed me now to pose a question it provoked. What was the connection with my life I sought that lay hidden, like the river beneath the pathless grassy vale indicated by the sign, and which flowed towards it.

Perhaps it was odd to attribute any kind of meaning to what may have been erected as a whimsical gesture, but then I always have been different. My life has never followed any accepted pattern of normality: several fellow travellers have described me as naive, stupid, impractical, lacking ambition, soft, crazy and 'not of this world'. I understood some of these opinions. When, as a schoolboy, others mocked me for my integrity, I didn't care. They often used me as a messenger, never sealing personal letters in the knowledge that I would not dream of reading them because I was 'stupidly honest'.

Few, if any, realised that I understood their thoughts, that this oddball could almost read their minds. It did not matter and I did not think less of them for their lack of insight.

My sojourn at the house on the avenue had lasted 37 years, 22 of them sharing the final years of a wonderful wife, sweetheart, friend, companion and lover, who made life so special for our family before gently departing into oblivion with the same grace that had enhanced every life she had touched.

Her gentle being was possessed by love and joy and tolerance. It sparkled with laughter, wisdom and impishness, and the music of her voice distilled all the beauty within.

2

THE IN-BETWEEN YEARS

On 2nd November 1927, north of the equator in the far eastern reaches of a country still part of the British Empire, a mother gave birth to twin boys. Only I survived. My twin brother, for whom no name is recorded, was said to have been stillborn. I am not aware that any documentation exists concerning his 'birth'. My own birthplace was correctly given on my birth certificate as Magwe, Burma, but my family moved to Mandalay soon after I was born, before I was old enough to remember. It was more than seventy years later when I discovered that two certificates of baptism had been issued from the Methodist Church, Mandalay, both with the number 761. One was dated 18th day of February 1933, the second dated 8th day of February 1934. The first was signed by a Mr Young and the second by a Mr Shepherd; both stated correctly that my place of abode was Mandalay. Much later I managed to unravel some reasons for the duplication of these documents and glean other details about my family — initially in March 1944, and more in March 2000, which helped me piece things together.

In March 1944 my mother penned three long, rambling, and sometimes incoherent letters to my mountain school, St Andrew's Colonial Homes. The letters were predominantly about my ancestry, and implored the teachers for their help to reclaim what she felt was my birthright (having failed in a previous attempt), through my titled great-grandfather, of which more later. However, I later came across another letter written to my parents from the school (which I was not meant to see) that explained how two Methodist ministers were deployed between 1931 and 1934 with the aim of gaining entry for me as a free boarder. The letter affirmed that my mother was a widow without means of support, and enclosed proof (why twice?!) that I had been baptized. My father had already died by this time, so the letter was addressed to my stepfather (Conrad G.) and expressed something more than frustration, which suggests that he had the means to pay and ought to do so.

The subject of my lineage in mother's letters sounded like a futile and desperate attempt to reclaim my 'heritage', but at least it did provide some information about my family that I had not known before.

Mother wrote that my father possessed written information passed to him by his own grandfather, who had walked away from a wealthy, titled and influential family in 1839. He rejected the name A..... C....., then enlisted on 18th February 1839 in London with the Madras Artillery under his 'adopted' name of Thomas Cribb and given the rank of sergeant major, Artillery Horse Brigade. This was not a post in the British Army, but rather in the private army run by the

East India Company. With no means of checking information about their 'first generation' recruit, his age was recorded as 'about twenty', so his actual date of birth may have been 1821 or 1822 depending on the month in which he was born (see below).

The newly named Thomas Cribb embarked with a large contingent of British service families aboard the 'Essex' in April 1839. This was before the Suez Canal was built so they sailed the long way round the Cape of Good Hope to join the established colony of British ex-pats in southern India.

Tom settled there and married Sarah, the daughter of a fellow soldier, and they had a son, Thomas Harry. Young Thomas followed his father — and gained the same rank — into the army (now the regular British Army after the East India Company had been dissolved in 1857).

Thomas Harry Cribb married Charlotte Florence Stephenson, the daughter of another officer in the same regiment, and his son, my father, Thomas Secluna Cribb was born on 15th May 1879 in Madras. I note that he would be 31 or 32 when his own grandfather died at the age of 88 or 89 on 8th May 1910.

During those 40 years, the Cribb family remained in or around the same areas of southern India and within the same community of British ex-pats. But after Britain 'acquired' the new colony of Burma in 1886, my grandfather was posted there to become Telegraph Master at Diamond Island off the south coast of what is now Myanmar. My father was seven when he moved there with his parents. He later followed his own father into the telegraph service.

Those sketchy details are all I possess about my antecedents. What happened after their arrival at Diamond Island is not much clearer, apart from what was written by my mother in those letters.

Mother was born Ethel Esperance West on 26th March 1893, at 55 Barr Street, Rangoon, Burma, to Henry Sherager West (of the Sussex or Surrey Regiment) and Jessy Agatha Pereira.

For the record, mother's parents were married on 7th June 1888 at the Roman Catholic Cathedral in Rangoon (now Yangon). My parents, Ethel West and Thomas Cribb, were married in the same city on 20th April 1911 at the Sagaw Karen Chapel, Bassein.

I was completely enveloped in a 'veil' as an infant, cosseted because of the traumatic circumstances of my birth; the whisper among adults was that I would be 'fey'. It would later prove that there was more than a grain of truth to the whispers, but it would be many years before it registered with me.

My father died suddenly in bed at around 3 a.m. on 23rd June 1931, aged 52. I was not yet four years old, so for all outward appearances everything at home seemed to go on as before. Home, set outside the town of Mandalay in central Burma, was comfortable and spacious, although perhaps because I was still cocooned from external interference, parenting seemed a bit remote. The two people closest to me were not my parents (or later my widowed mother and stepfather), but rather my nanny, or ayah, and the man who conveyed me in a carriage to and from the convent school in the city. The cooking staff, though they served food at every meal and occupied and worked in buildings at the rear of the house, remain in the shadow of my memory. Yet I still savour a few details of my early life in Mandalay.

I attended St Joseph's school and remember being happy there. Even though it was a convent school, teaching staff were not religious sisters. My favourite teacher called me 'lighthouse' because I was bright, had fair hair and, it seemed to me, I had a cheerful and helpful attitude. My daily trip to school — in a horse-drawn carriage — took me across a wooden bridge high above a small river just a short distance from home, but alas the rest of the journey never registered with me.

However indistinct it remains, I still remember a car journey undertaken at night at about this time because it was on a lonely road through the dense jungle accompanied by tales of the spirits that dwelt there and warnings about how one should avoid entering deep into the jungle at night. I cannot recall my mother being present, where the place was, or the purpose of the journey. But I do remember going to bed that evening far from the family home in a strange house surrounded by marshy fields and being lulled to sleep by the croaking of a thousand frogs, a musical chorus I loved.

The only other journey that made an impression on me during these years took me hundreds of kilometres down the Irrawaddy River (famous as the Road to Mandalay in

Kipling's poem) to visit some family friends in Rangoon, where I was escorted around a huge Pagoda before sailing back home.

My memories of these early years may seem sketchy but most details up to the age of seven were blurred in my mind by events that would take me away from my protected life in Burma. My change of life would be so dramatic that even the little I once imagined I knew, faded into a dark place.

The period between my father's death in June 1931, and October 1934 introduced a new element into the family home in the form of a portly white man. Though he registered in my mind as physically large, his presence remained indistinct because he constantly appeared and disappeared from the house, creating a feeling of unease in me. It had nothing to do with him being a stranger because I was generally at ease with most people. Perhaps being born fey was kicking in at an early stage. History would prove that these negative vibrations were correct. I was never told what the rotund man was doing around the house and I didn't ask. The facts of the matter only registered a year or two later when I learned that an arrangement had been made between my mother and the man. He was to become my stepfather. My departure from the house prior to their union had been part of the agreement, and I would come to realise that the only person he wanted in his life was his new wife.

Mother prepared me for the upcoming change in my life over a long period of time. She told me that I would be going away to school (I was not aware of what kind of school, where it was, or for how long I should be there), and was not to worry because it was 'for your own good'. Those four words were repeated so often that I eventually told her that I was not at all concerned, which was true, because in my innocence I believed it. What could possibly happen that would harm me? How wonderful is a young boy's faith in the milk of human kindness when offered by his mother.

When left alone — which seemed to be often, as I was a quiet and contemplative child — I was happy to occupy my time outside as there were open fields on one side of the house and also across the traffic-free unmade road in front. Saying I was happy may be a slight exaggeration because Burma always felt alien to me, but deliberate physical alienation from everything Burmese may have been just one reason. Something within me longed for contact with all things English, such as seasonal changes, mist, gentle rain, cloudy skies, with the easy comfort of a familiar language and English customs. I cannot say why someone born away from Britain would feel all these things, but that something within me was real and powerful.

My older sister Charlotte married before I was two years old, and my brother Tom was just two years her junior, which indicates the age gap between me and my Cribb siblings. I belonged to another generation. As though to further increase the distance between us, my sister was born in Diamond Island, hundreds of kilometres away off the southwest coast of Burma. Tom was born in Moulmein (now Mawlamyine), further still, near the border with Thailand, formerly Siam.

Despite Mother's preparations for my departure, I had little warning that, aged six, life was to change so radically. I did not know where I would be going or for how long, or that my journey would take me across the sea, or that the time and distance to my destination would be so great. Nor did I know that I would never return to Burma or to the family home.

With the aid of documentation I obtained much later in life, I am able to state accurately the important dates of my departure from Mandalay.

A letter to St Andrew's Colonial Homes — significantly written by the same Mr Shepherd who signed my second baptism certificate — stated that I would leave Mandalay on 5th October 1934, and that after sailing down the Irrawaddy to Rangoon, I would embark for Calcutta on 9th October. The letter appears to confirm the successful culmination of my 'parents" three years of effort, with Mr Shepherd's help, to have me accepted as a free boarder.

What stands out most clearly from that time was how my mother reacted when the moment came for my departure. She wept uncontrollably.

I attempted to console her by repeating what had been drummed into me for so long. 'It's for my own good,' I said. 'Don't worry.'

My belief in what I said was total.

A telegram, sent on ahead to the school, simply stated "Cribb arriving Calcutta October 11th". The date of school admission was recorded as 17th October, so the entire journey (allowing for four or five days in quarantine) must have taken eight or nine days.

Like most things that happened in those years, my memory of the journey remains hazy. I remember travelling sedately from Mandalay on the river steamer, calling at several places on the Irrawaddy, towns that I could only identify later in life by referring to a map.

My brother Tom accompanied me from Mandalay to Rangoon, and then took me to the ocean-going vessel bound for Calcutta (now Kolkata). I never saw my brother again.

I recall little about the sailing, just that I was seasick on deck. I offered to clean it up, and remember being impressed when someone ran out a hose and washed it overboard in a trice. On arrival in Calcutta I was met by a uniformed police officer who told me that he was an old boy from St Andrew's who had volunteered to escort me the rest of the way.

The rail journeys were easier to remember because since boyhood I have always liked trains. From Sealdah Station in Calcutta I travelled across the Great Ganges Plain to Siliguri, before boarding the famous British built D.H.R. or Darjeeling Himalayan Railway, a narrow-gauge track that wound its way in slow, wide sweeps up the densely wooded foothills of the Himalayas to Kalimpong. Dubbed locally as the Toy Train, it took eight hours to complete a journey that can now be done by car in just over an hour.

3

EARLY MEMORIES

I was met at Kalimpong station by a car and driver, who deposited me at the foot of a hill that was to become very familiar over the next few years. There were various school buildings and a number of cottages on the steep hill above the road. I looked up to a church, then up many, many steps in uneven groups of five or eight towards a hospital. Waiting to conduct me up there were two nurses in uniform. When they approached, my immediate reaction was to protest that I was not sick and did not need their help, and when they took an arm each I yelled and bellowed in protest. One of the nurses explained that it was just a school routine to check every newcomer before being allowed into a cottage. I remember wondering why this had not been explained earlier because, I thought, I am an intelligent boy and always willing to listen.

I steeled myself for a few days' quarantine. In fact, my stay in the Steele Memorial Hospital was generally pleasant, and I found everyone kind and helpful. The shocks were to come on discharge.

I later learned that the hospital was mainly staffed by former pupils who were training to be nurses and supervised by qualified doctors and managers imported from 'home', i.e. Britain.

Following a few days' observation, I was ready to be sent to my new home: Assam Cottage. I would live there until I was 15.

The first surprise was when I asked for the return of my shoes, only to be told I would not need them because everyone at school was barefoot, whether they were fully paid boarders, part paid, or free boarders.

I picked my way down the hill to Assam Cottage in anticipation of my first night in 'the big dorm', chosen because the free bed was nearest to the cottage housemother. She thought it would be a comforting position for the new boy. Alas for good intentions and not understanding how boys think. It did not work out.

That night, when the dormitory light was switched off, a hurricane lantern was left just inside the doorway so I would not be in total darkness in this strange place. All was peaceful until I heard what I believed were wolves howling just outside the window. I had never heard that sound before, but do remember being told that wolves howled at the moon, so all thoughts of sleep departed. I lay still, tense with fear, not aware then that what I could hear was the howling of jackals, another animal new to me.

Before I could settle, a dark figure wearing on his head the square metal tin normally used to store spoons darted through the door, snatched the lantern and left me in pitch darkness. Already in a tense state, I howled like a banshee until others arrived, who switched on the lights and calmed me down. It was a while before I managed to drop off.

The following night I joined other boys of my own age in the small dorm. The events of the previous evening came back to haunt me because the boys had all heard my yelling, and marked me out as one ripe for torment.

The bedtime routine started at 7 p.m. when the youngest washed, brushed their teeth and got into their pyjamas, followed by older groups from both dormitories at half-hourly intervals. Everyone was in bed by 9 p.m. for lights out. School grounds were patrolled by night watchmen, usually local inhabitants, and any pupil caught outside at night was liable for expulsion. I later heard that the curfew was designed to avoid illicit meetings between the sexes in the night hours.

We were summonsed for school by a large gong that hung outside a school block. I loved its deep resonance from the first day I heard it; the sound echoed and rolled around the hillsides for huge distances. Whoever designed and crafted it had done a wonderful job.

Everyone ran to be in time for assembly at 8.30 a.m., for late arrival was frowned upon and punished by detention or lines or, if repeated too often, the cane. Accompanied by a member of staff, I followed suit and made my way to form three of the junior school on that first cold morning. I was instantly dismissed as too advanced for the class, so I was moved up to form four where I spent a few minutes before being moved on once again to the first form of the senior school. I was deposited in class 1B where I would remain for the last few weeks of term. I was told that it was a temporary class and that I would start in 1A at the beginning of the following school year in 1935.

The rapid change of scene — new country, new school, new rules, new companions, different speech intonations if not a completely new language, the enormous expanse of snowcapped mountains to the north, the large mountain kites wheeling around in the sky, the howling jackals at night — all served to confuse me and was all too much to swallow in one gulp. These details barely registered when I was first hurled into life at St Andrew's Colonial Homes (or KPG as it was known to pupils), because my head was spinning with the shock of the new. It was a marked contrast to the quiet, sheltered home I had left behind. It was too unreal, just a dream.

The boys at school wore the simple, classic uniform of shorts and shirt, with jackets for winter — but legs bare from the knees down, no matter what the season. Every garment was produced in the tailoring department run by Miss Coutts from seemingly endless runs of plain grey fabric, so uniformity was maintained throughout. It would take many years for me to register the 'Scottishness' of those frugal arrangements and the reasoning behind them. Apparently the founder, Dr Graham, grew up in an open country area of Scotland where all the children ran around shoeless. He believed it was 'healthy' — and cheaper — so had adopted the same reasoning for his school set in another open remote area that reminded him of home. Never mind that we were in the foothills of the Himalayas.

Whatever the reason, going shoeless created great difficulty for newcomers, who could always be spotted picking their way carefully over rough terrain. The school was isolated — about 400 miles from the nearest large city, Calcutta — so the roads were unmade, and usually hard and stony. The closest habitation was the small village of Kalimpong, two miles down the hill (which has now grown into a large, sprawling town).

Walking without shoes in October was bad enough, but I would later learn that stepping over hard, frosty ground barefoot in winter would be a shock to the system. Journeys were made by foot as no mechanised form of transport existed, so whether a journey was a mile or ten miles or more, boys were required to walk, or more frequently run because time was precious.

The school buildings stood on a flat piece of land, with the cottages — each housing around 30 children, aged from seven to 15 — widely scattered at various levels across the hillsides: boys' cottages to one side, the girls' straddling the hill on the other.

Storage facilities in the cottage were basic. A wall lined with triple level, open-fronted cubes two feet square served as cupboards for every personal possession, including clothing, so nothing could be hidden or kept private. I soon learned that real or perceived valuables left in those cubes would disappear and were never seen again. Fortunately, even at such a tender age, I never attached value to possessions because it always seemed unimportant.

The day began at 6 a.m. at the sound of a loud ringing bell. Beds were stripped, mattresses turned, sheets and blankets replaced, under the watchful eye of a housemother or her assistant. Usually these proceedings took no more than five minutes before quickly moving on to the work rota. The theory was that washing yourself came before starting listed jobs, but I remember how icy water put me off from ever washing my face, so perhaps I never washed very much.

At the time it never registered that an isolated community so far from civilisation would actually have running water on tap — even the icy cold sort — or that every cottage had electricity and flush toilets as standard. But why would it. There was little time for anything to make an impression because it took me at least three years to recover from the shock of being dropped into this new way of life.

The Scottish way of life ensured that every minute of school was filled with activity — religious, physical and cerebral — which was grounded in the belief that the three Rs alone were inadequate as an education. Children needed to accomplish other tasks demanded in real life, such as cooking, cleaning, gardening, laundry, and generally helping out wherever needed. The reasoning is quite sound but it left very little time to enjoy the beautiful environment.

The physical aspects of school life revolved around cleaning, and there was plenty of it. The system was simple. Every junior was paired with a senior on a rota that changed weekly. Dormitories had to be cleaned every day — as did all the other rooms in the house — the stove lit and breakfast cooked (always porridge) by a pair who rose at five o'clock. Dining room duty required tables to be laid and later cleaned, and then there was scullery duty, pantry service (for the staff) and so on. Everything inside and outside the cottages was maintained by the boys. Washable items like dirty towels were sanitised in the huge, round cast iron boiler that hung above a log fire in the outhouse, then put through a large hand-operated mangle before being pegged out on a washing line. The floors were bare polished wood (except for staff rooms) that required cleaning and re-polishing daily; matching wood panelling needed similar treatment. Everything was inspected on completion.

The most hated job was lavatory cleaning. Our cottage had four doorless cubicles in a row, with toilet pans topped with wood strips fastened on the rims. The floor had a solid, impervious stone finish and there was one door separating the cubicles from the dressing rooms that had a high mesh grill at the opposite end open to the fresh air. The arrangement might seem perfectly adequate and sensible, but boys are not sensible. It was always a real mess, with faeces on the seats and urine an inch deep so that everyone was forced to stand three feet away and aim at the pan. Cleaning it all up in bare feet with just a bucket of water, phenol, a scrubbing brush and a cloth was not a pleasant job.

As important as these practical activities were, they were not allowed to interfere with spiritual enrichment. Pupils had to attend both morning and evening prayers following breakfast and tea (the evening meal always being called tea!). Evening prayers usually required the regurgitation of randomly drawn texts from that morning's prayers, so I developed my own system of recall. For instance, I would remember "The just shall live by faith: Hebrews ten, thirty-eight", by making it (almost) rhyme, or inserting (in my mind) a hook on which to hang it. It was just a game, helping me escape from both the real and imagined terrors around me.

So much for the misery imposed by the masters. Eventually the school bullies caught up with me, and I had to endure the taunts of some tough, streetwise boys. They loved to pick on the quiet, innocent boy that I was, and found it easy to knock about and fool because I was utterly clueless about the realities of life in the new environment. With little time to think about anything except survival, the next four years became a minor hell. How did I deal with the situation? Eventually I learned to conceal what I felt.

Those first few years at St Andrew's for a young innocent boy were to prove crucial to whether I would withstand the onslaught or live to become withdrawn and solitary for life. My daytime fears were frequently played out as vivid nightmares, one of which repeated itself several times over the following months until I taught myself to wake up the moment it began, a useful trick for life. That nightmare has never faded from memory. A dark, swirling shape would flow into the dormitory from the end window, grow rapidly and fill the room until it smothered me. I would always wake up just before I succumbed. Later, I learned to levitate in my dreams, willing myself to leave the ground by mind power until I rose above everything and could see the world spread out below. I felt safe up there, but was also fully aware that my dreams allowed only a temporary escape from daytime fears.

I was so preoccupied with the changed circumstances of my life during the 1930s that global history completely passed me by. I was not to know that the world outside the school in the foothills of the Himalayas was in flux, that Adolf Hitler (who?) had already started moves towards world domination, and that World War Two would soon erupt.

4

LIFE IN THE HILLS

I had no choice but to get used to life in the foothills of the Himalayas, miles from all habitation except for the village down the hill and a few scattered dwellings. But looking on the positive side, the view from the school was spectacular, with the snow-capped mountains to the north and steep hillsides plunging down to the valleys on the south side. The air that blew across the roof of the world was pure, fresh and very cold. Despite this, dormitory windows were never closed, so icy — often frozen — bed sheets were standard in winter. The cottages were unheated, but the dining room had two large wood-burning fireplaces, one at each end, used on special occasions in the depths of winter.

For those who never left the place throughout their schooldays, either because they had no homes of their own (supported free boarders) or because their homes were too far away (me!), it was profound isolation from the realities of a harsh world. Acclimatisation to any form of institution, benevolent or otherwise, and distanced from 'civilisation' for 10 or 12 years, created problems for a proportion of school-leavers, especially the girls. Many had arrived as infants, started life at the purpose-built Lucia King cottage, and never knew life outside the school. Isolation from the rest of the world and its distractions was an advantage for some, but possessed a sting in the tail for others who lived there for many years and found it difficult to adjust to life outside.

A former headmistress of the junior school (herself a former pupil) told me in the year 2000 that historical evidence existed to prove that institutionalisation took hold of numerous 'old girls' in later life, who longed to return because they missed their 'home' so much.

Despite the demands on our precious time — rotas, cleaning, etc — we managed to fit in moments of wicked activity, such as quick raids on local farms that grew oranges, maize, pineapples and other fresh and edible delicacies. Some of these forays often needed long, fast runs downhill over great distances, with the danger of being discovered either by the farmers or school staff. The former threw large clods of earth at the flying figures, the latter inflicted punishment with the cane, detention or in extreme cases, expulsion.

At least the activity kept us warm and fit. It also kept us hungry. Although school meals were fresh and nourishing enough to sustain the body, I always needed more than the average boy because I was at least a head taller than boys even a couple of years older.

It took several years before I discovered the origins of the majority of other boys. By that time I really did not care who they were as long as they did not hit me. Some were born of Scottish or English fathers and local mothers, who worked as pickers on the local tea plantations, which perhaps accounted for their lack of stature. Their very existence was the reason that Dr Graham created the school, to care for these often abandoned children — most white plantation men already had wives and children back home in Britain. Somehow he felt personally responsible for the offspring of his fellow countrymen, who constituted about 98% of all students. By 1934 most pupils arrived from established backgrounds with parents holding responsible jobs and able to pay for their education.

Dr Graham's achievements between building the first cottage for six children in 1900 and my arrival in 1934 could be described as spectacular, verging on the miraculous. Apart from 18 cottages (seven for girls and 11 for boys), by this time the school also boasted its own hospital, swimming pool, farms (vegetable, cattle, poultry and pigs) that supplied all the meat, milk and butter, a bakery, a church, dwellings for senior staff, a huge playing field lower down the hill, a tailoring department, tennis courts, a music hall, and the Jarvie Hall complete with clock tower that replicated the appearance and chimes of Big Ben. Additionally, he had acquired the Birkmyre Hostel in Calcutta as a jumping-off place for school-leavers who were without parental support and needed help acclimatising to city life.

I later learned that Dr Graham terrified every influential or wealthy person he met because he refused to take no for an answer when he was looking for donations. He managed to lever large sums out of most people, 'rewarding' them by naming various buildings or grounds in their honour. With James Purdie, another Scot, as school superintendent, the organisation ran like a well-oiled machine. Just how much was done by this kind and wonderful back-up person was kept under wraps while I was a pupil, and only revealed to me much later in life.

These incredible advances at the school could never have happened without the services of numerous volunteers — teachers, cottage aunties, key farm and hospital workers, office workers, and tailoring or supervisory staff recruited from Britain. Most worked for their keep during their stint of a year or two, which enabled the school to put the saved expenditure into expansion. These arrangements had some obvious disadvantages such as the inevitable frequent turnover of teachers. St Andrew's Colonial Homes was publicised in the UK as being founded on Christian principles, so volunteers often arrived filled with religious zeal. However, a significant minority of houseparents proved to be frustrated spinsters with little understanding of children. Other teachers who stayed on permanently proved to be wonderful, helpful and inspirational. They kept the overall standard of formal education high so that those fortunate to have ability and a desire to learn, left school with enhanced opportunities to progress in life.

5

FINDING WAYS TO SURVIVE

I learned quite early that survival could never be dependent on others, but had to come from within. I explored various ways to do this, not all feasible or sensible because I fell victim either to school rules, to boys with more experience, or to a combination of events that were new to me. As a beginner in that exploratory field (in a way I was like a child straight out of the cradle) it was to take some time, but patience was always one of my strengths. My thought processes may have been lauded many years later as lateral thinking.

The process was painfully slow, and I suffered a great deal of pain along the way. Getting used to physical pain was easier than the mind games practised on the unwary by experts in the field. When those experts were older, bigger, streetwise and cruel, it was tough. There was no one I could turn to for help. I was on my own.

Whenever I became involved in an incident not of my choosing, 'slow' William inevitably became the scapegoat simply because I was the last to run away. One member of house staff blamed me for everything that happened. If I angrily identified the real culprit, I was regarded as a sneak (and thumped), so that had to be ruled out very quickly.

Despite my age and inexperience I began finding positives from the situation. I discovered that inflicted pain teaches you about yourself and how to live with it (not always easy). I sometimes escaped by climbing a tree, sitting in the fork of a branch and gazing around at the snow-covered mountains, or looking down into the valleys and wondering what life was really all about. Even in those early years a philosophical temperament was developing.

I never wanted to join any kind of group, nor would I automatically do what everyone else did, such as smoke banned cigarettes as most boys did when out of the sight of teachers. I did my own thing regardless of peer pressures or fear of being shut out from their other activities. I wanted to be my own person. I refused to do what went against my principles or what I disliked, and was almost stupidly stubborn about it. However, my attitude did not prevent me from considering others who were too scared to battle it out, and I often stood with them and took further wallopings. Just how daft can one be?

This learning curve was a long, slow one, and must have taken at least three or four years because I was content to be a plodder. Fortunately, even though I was at least a year younger than everyone in the class, I found schoolwork easy and I could get by with little effort. Strangely, in later life I have always regretted finding it so because it can become a disadvantage when really hard mental effort is demanded.

I gradually learned that negative thoughts should be dismissed quickly, a lesson that was to last for the rest of my life.

6

THE PLUS RATIO

It took a couple of years to realise that there was so much about the school to be celebrated: clean air, good fresh food, some incredible teachers, beds with the most comfortable mattresses I have ever slept on, a variety of good books from classics to tales of derring-do and schoolboy yarns from English public schools, and the most beautiful vistas one could ever wish to look upon every day. Another plus was unlimited space. There were woods above and below the school where we found trees where we could construct secret hiding places against the hillsides using boughs and shrubs to conceal entrances so skilfully that no one but boys knew they existed.

My second period of quarantine, which began the moment I had completed the first, was a six-month ban from the swimming pool, another standard procedure for newcomers. It is astonishing how a ban on any activity can bring on a longing to participate, especially when everyone else seems to be enjoying themselves. After months of gazing longingly at others running along and diving or jumping in the water, the day arrived when permission was given for me to join the fun.

I was so excited at my first venture into the pool. I had already visualised running along the side and leaping into the water. To save time that day I wore swimming trunks under my shorts and set off at speed to arrive first at the swimming baths. In my eagerness, I blanked out every other thought as I hurled myself as far into the water as possible. But there were a couple of problems: I had forgotten to remove my clothes, forgotten to shower, forgotten that I was now in the deep end, and last but not least, forgotten that I could not swim. I sank, then I floated up, I sank again at least three more times before a senior boy leapt in fully clothed to rescue me. At no time did it ever cross my mind that I could drown. I just found it exhilarating.

After I was dragged out of the water and got changed, my wet clothes were run up the flagpole and a photograph taken that made the school magazine. Three weeks later I won a prize for swimming the breadth of the pool.

With teachers such as D.D. Scott, H.T. Bamfield, Miss G. Hasting, Miss Oldham and other inspirational tutors, a child had to be uncaring, ignorant or incapable of learning not to benefit from their teaching. They were ready to give whatever time was needed to go over, again and again if requested, the subjects they taught, and it was obvious that they really cared. I now know it was more than just a job for them.

But it was not all sweetness and light in the classroom. Punishment and harsh treatment were meted out by teachers in ways that would not be allowed today, and there were a couple of staff who rejoiced in 'handing it out'. The really cruel one was the headmaster who came from Ruthin in Wales, who had a row of elegant canes carefully calibrated from slender to heavy. They were not mere showpieces. He did not discriminate between the genders, beating boys and girls with equal gusto. I eventually joined the club. I must have kept myself under the radar before then.

There were several decent and helpful boys too, but help always came with reservations because nothing was free, especially when the most powerful bullies were at the top. The brothers Billy and Peter were in Assam Cottage at the right time to act as useful guardians during a difficult period for me. They discovered that I had developed a strong back for my age and could carry them (in turn) for horse-and-rider battles. There were no rules, but the general idea was to completely knock over opponents or dislodge other riders. Horse and rider could both push, pull or tug at any part of the body, but I would charge at opponents and they invariably gave ground or keeled over. I enjoyed the roughhousing without malicious intent because it gave vent to a lot of inhibitions.

Though Peter was the younger brother, he was physically taller and stronger than Billy. Both were fearless. One mealtime, when staff were absent, Peter showed his mettle. I was being badly treated by the senior boy in the cottage who was sitting at the head of the table when Peter asked him to stop teasing me. It amused the senior because he was at least two years older than Peter, but the younger boy repeated his request. The resulting fist fight was remembered by all for years to come. It lasted for over half an hour, and took the scrappers around the dining room, through the scullery, the bathroom and kitchen and back into the dining room. They were both bruised and exhausted, with no winner or loser, but Peter had made his point. I was never again troubled by anyone in the cottage. By the time the brothers moved on, I had become stronger and better able to stand my ground.

I remember two other boys who arrived in Assam, stayed for a year then departed, something that seemed to happen on a regular basis. One, named John Walters, was a strong, black American boy, the other an Armenian who rejoiced in the name of Haik Thaddeus, and who was also physically powerful enough to quell insults, that for some reason often described him as a fish. The two new boys were decent, kind and helpful, and we became friends. I was sorry when they departed.

As I grew older, and stronger, I was in a position to help other boys who needed it, boys like Alec C., Abe Cohen and Jones. The first two were small, weak and unable to defend themselves. However, my efforts to aid them proved useless and I too was beaten up. Abe left the school within a few months; Alec stayed on and spent much of his time trying unsuccessfully to hide from bullies. Jones proved to be more courageous. On his return from a long Christmas break, his little case was seized by bullies who threatened to break it open if he did not unlock it to reveal the 'goodies' from home.

I told him, 'Stand back to back with me and we'll fight together.'

And that's what we did. Even though we both finished tired and bruised, and the case was eventually broken open and the contents looted, at least the others had to battle for their ill-gotten gains.

7

CAMPING TALES

Annual visits to the valley gave us opportunities to bend school rules. With no formal lessons, less supervision, more time and new territory to explore, everyone rejoiced in the freedom from prying eyes.

I went with the flow, enjoying the sound of running water and the escape from school discipline, and often joined groups venturing along woodland paths on the fringes of the river bank because it felt safer than being alone. As an exuberant and devil-may-care 12-year-old I was happy to join the other boys in dangerously wild and crazy escapades, but drew the line when other kids' behaviour went too far, such as hurting others.

I can clearly recall several teenage adventures at the River Rilli. The railway followed the line of the river for some distance before crossing a bridge high above the ravine. The sleepers were unevenly spaced, each gap varied from between one and three feet or more and presented a challenge to barefoot boys racing across from one side to the other. Any slip would have meant a fall of at least 90 feet into the ravine below. On one occasion three or four lads were caught in the middle of the bridge when a train appeared from around the bend. It was a case of either swinging down into the steelwork below the bridge or death by locomotive. Fortunately no hot coals or ashes were discharged at that point, something that never crossed anyone's mind at the time. The boys lived to carry out more dares.

Stealing a ride by clinging on top of a loaded (open) carrier on the rope railway that came down the hill to the station was no less dangerous. The rope (similar to a ski lift) spanned the river and the extra weight of even a light boy took the carrier perilously close to the surface of the water. I tried it once but was so scared I never did it again. It was a stunt that would have led to expulsion from school if caught.

The Rilli in full spate could be dangerous if you wanted to cross to the opposite bank. Never more than three or four feet deep but with treacherous slippery rocks, it was almost impossible to regain a foothold if you slipped. Once I came close to ending my short life there. I was trying to cross to the opposite bank when I was swept down the fast-flowing river, fully aware that around two more bends the Rilli joined the River Teesta, a deep stretch of water full of undercurrents. Battered and bruised against what seemed like every rock in the river, I spotted a figure on the bend ahead and yelled out to him. He ran to the bank, picked up a long branch from the side and held it out. I grabbed it so violently that I almost pulled in my rescuer. Fortunately he held his ground and pulled me ashore.

I was later told that crossings should always be done by several people holding hands to steady each other, never alone when it was running strongly. I learned my lesson and escaped with no more than a few painful bruises.

Sadly, one young Kalimpong schoolboy was drowned in the Rilli during a camping holiday. He was missing at mealtime one evening and searches around the area came up blank. It took at least another hour to find his lifeless body wedged out of sight under a rock close to the far bank. The mystery of how he got stuck there was never solved.

The plantation manager from across the river once asked for help to build a temporary diversionary angled dam on his riverbank, which made an interesting change for the boys. It was a warm sunny day so it was an enjoyable experience. Partway through the operation a bronzed young Englishman in shirt and shorts came walking along the bank. When asked to help, he duly obliged. When it was complete, the manager gave all the boys a few coppers and did the same for the young man who thanked him politely as he carefully pocketed the coins.

The following day, another bright, sunny one, a short train was seen travelling slowly along the riverbank with an open, awning-covered carriage at the rear. A family of four — father, mother and two children — were sitting at a table enjoying breakfast. The father was the bronzed dam-helper of the previous day. They waved and smiled and everyone returned their greetings. Enquiries revealed that he was the district superintendent, sufficiently important to be awarded a private train for his use during tours of the area. What a wonderfully modest and courteous man he must have been. He certainly left everyone he had met feeling better about the human race, and specifically about Englishmen abroad. Not all expatriates were as helpful.

Once, during a walk through the woods, a schoolboy asked why I was the only non-smoker in the group. The answer was simple: I didn't want to. The other nine boys all had lighted cigarettes in their hands. One proffered his to me, but I waved it away. With help from a companion he then attempted to forcibly place it between my lips only to get a swipe across his own mouth. Instantly I was set upon by the whole gang and the fight that ensued left me with cut, swollen lips and a face that reflected a severe pounding. But at least I had the satisfaction of seeing several other faces looking worse for wear. I derived some pleasure from this experience and the new respect from my fellows, and vowed that no one would ever compel me to smoke.

8

VISITORS TO KALIMPONG

Because of its unique location, its proximity to what were then the Tibetan, Nepalese and Bhutanese borders, the fact that it was in India — still a British Colony — combined with the growing influence of its founder, the school attracted many visitors.

Some were fascinating personal friends of Dr Graham, such as the leading Bengali philosopher Dr Rabindranath Tagore. Others included missionaries and preachers curious about the school, friends of the founder, or influential political figures from Bengal or India at large.

The son of Bhutan's Prime Minister, Rajah Dorji, would sometimes arrive with members of his father's staff (with a large Alsatian dog in tow) to play football with the boys on the Ronaldshay Park, where St Andrew's had three football pitches and a running track.

Missionaries like Colonel Coldstream (his rank in British Intelligence) were always made welcome, especially by the schoolchildren. C.C. was tall and strong, with a cheerful personality to match his stature. As he stood before the preacher, the minister in him radiated everything that was best about religion. He never arrived without his gigantic yet gentle dog, an animal that was so strong he was able to carry children on his back.

Others who came to preach sermons at Sunday services made me shudder. I listened with horror to one who thundered from the pulpit about hellfire and damnation for unbelievers, compounding his 'message' by exhorting 'all sinners here' to come forward and confess their sins. How, I wondered, could anyone be so incredibly stupid when addressing young innocent children, and attempt to scare them into accepting religious belief on the basis of fear. Looking at scared faces around me, the only feeling I had was anger.

Fortunately some of the other preachers were more aware that their congregations were composed of children, even when religious zeal carried them along. One minister from a church in Calcutta turned out to be a great speaker and certainly kept everyone fully awake because he combined his message with humour and stories suitable for our ages.

Several Everest expeditions travelled through Kalimpong — in 1933, 1936 and 1938, with a reconnaissance expedition in 1935. I can still remember the 1938 expedition led by Bill Tilman. The team included Shipton and Smythe (the Telegraph correspondent), with Warren, Oliver and two others returning from another attempt on the summit. They sat in the chancel in their climbing kit as two of them read the lessons. The first photographs of what was purported to be a Yeti's footprints were taken on that expedition. One of the team was a young Sherpa Tensing who had also travelled with the 1935 expedition; unknown at the time but later to be one of the first two climbers to reach the summit.

During the long school holidays at Christmas the handful of boys remaining — myself included — who were usually based at Assam Cottage, took camping trips to the Rilli at a point close to where it flowed into the wider and deeper Teesta River. It was real camping: three or four tents with up to eight boys in each, sleeping on the ground in sleeping bags. With the river to one side and woods on the other, cooking done on a makeshift construction on the sand, and shrubbery in the woods as a lavatory, it worked quite well. A major advantage was that for several years we had a cook who produced all the meals, a real plus for the boys, who turned it into something special for a week or 10 days. He was a grizzled, tough old man nicknamed 'Lo Lo' by the boys after his muttering and mumbling while he worked. With hands like leather, he rearranged red-hot embers in the fire with his bare fingers as the boys watched in wonder, and produced special food that had never appeared at any school meal I had ever eaten.

9

MOMOS, CASTOR OIL AND RUNAWAYS

Life in Kalimpong was never dull, especially when, like all boys my age, I found distractions away from the routine, from bullies and from the realities of a 'crowded' existence in one small house.

I was forced to go along with some groups who were out for adventure because they saw themselves as experts on the surrounding areas, such as sneaking down to the village for momos, which satisfied at least one need: food. School rules outlawed such excursions, so caution and speed were necessary. The shop that sold these odd little dumplings in soup was in a building up a flight of steep steps on the edge of the village. The dish, perhaps Tibetan or Bhutanese in origin, was served piping hot in bowls and incredibly cheap, each portion costing about tuppence. The meat inside the dumplings could have come from any animal at all, but who cared — it was a tasty little snack.

On one occasion a boy spotted a member of staff approaching the shop. The only solution was to exit rapidly by leaping from the rear window and running like the wind back up the hill.

However, we didn't need to go to shops for tasty food. Finding strange fruit or berries on the hillsides or in the woods tempted the boys to try them, often making them ill. A variety of plum was christened 'snotty' plum because of its consistency and appearance, and I could never decide whether it tasted odd or just awful, so left it alone. I tried several other unusual wild fruits but never found any that were so tempting that I wanted more. In the process of these trials many boys were quite sick and cottage staff treated them with doses of castor oil — horrible, smelly stuff that made me retch the moment it issued from the bottle.

Unfortunately, not all these dietary experiments in wild foods resulted in curable illnesses. There were one or two really bad consequences from 'unknown causes' leading to hospitalisation, even death. I suspected that eating berries from poisonous plants may have been responsible, but no one ever knew for certain; if they did, the pupils were never told. A lot of things happened that were never explained or even mentioned. New pupils came and quickly left, boys and girls fell ill, were hospitalised, and not all recovered. One girl was unwell in class, sent to hospital, returned to school the next day, fell ill again, went back to hospital and never returned. The school grapevine reported that she had died.

School discipline was another area that we feared. It always seemed to me that boys were more harshly treated than girls. Perhaps they were harder to control, or cottage staff, who were all female, did not really understand boys.

Most runaways were boys who could not cope. Some returned, but odd ones just disappeared and were never seen again.

On one occasion I was severely punished by the housemother at Assam when I accidentally backed into a giant sunflower and broke its stem. She leaned out of the window and screamed at me to go upstairs where she was brandishing a heavy walking stick. In her rage, she brought it down savagely on my upturned hands. The damage to my palms was so bad that it shocked her. She was uncertain about what to do, so she put me to bed. My hands were very painful and swollen for several days; one wrist took years to heal properly. That memory never left me, and horrified me so much that I never felt able to forgive her.

In an almost unlimited amount of open space, accidents were inevitable, and broken limbs not uncommon, usually as a result of climbing trees. I had one or two major falls, the most serious of which was when I was preparing to jump off the parapet surrounding the swimming baths. I lost balance, but instinctively hurled myself beyond the wall to avoid a deeper drop. I landed heavily on a grassy bank and was unable to help myself for some time, not sure whether I had actually lost consciousness for a while. No one else was present to witness it or offer help.

Kite-flying was also responsible for several boys falling out of trees, after they tried to retrieve precious handmade kites from high branches. Young Matthew Douglas enjoyed climbing. Nicknamed 'cat', he volunteered to reach seemingly impossible branches, but despite being warned on one occasion to forget a kite that landed at the outer extremity of a high branch, he insisted on climbing up. The bough broke and he fell to the ground. He was taken to hospital but died the same day.

Leaping from high places was a dangerous sport, and most leaps were the subject of a dare. Sometimes following heavy rain, landslips would appear on the hillside. We discovered one about a mile from school that lent itself to another dangerous game — seeing who could leap farthest beyond the bottom end of it. I found myself drawn into the crazy pastime. Remembering that the area below was littered with rocks and rough lumps from the earth slide, leaping involved a fast run up to the top to clear the obstacles. Attempting it in bare feet, the exercise bordered on lunacy. Bruises and cuts on feet and legs along with the odd broken toe were the commonest injuries, but miraculously little else that could be seen or admitted.

I sometimes took things beyond common sense as a protest against bullying. Running away from a group of boys, I would run very fast up a hill, turn around and leap on them from a great height. I never thought about the pain I might feel if it went wrong, but it certainly had the effect of scattering them and warning them for next time. They dubbed me as crazy and unpredictable, and I responded by even greater acts of madness. It was an effective, if sometimes painful, method of deterrent.

The school kitchen was no less safe. An incident involving a pot of soup caused severe burns and a lifelong problem for an Assam boy. The pot in question was a huge, oval, iron cooking utensil with a large handle at each end. For some reason it was on the floor, and two boys were larking about when one backed into it and sat down in the boiling liquid. The severe burns healed in due course, but he became subject to 'fitting', or epileptic seizures, for several years and died around the age of 19.

Around this time (I must have been about 14), I came under the scrutiny of the headmaster, either directly or via the 'kind' reporting of house staff. I remember a period of at least three years when the head caned me on a regular basis. I rebelled against what I saw as unfairness, which only led to more beatings. I did not have the sense to lie low; I fought back and took yet more canings. I joked that I had acquired a permanent range of hills across my bottom. Even so, the severity of the beatings was not a matter for joking. The head really enjoyed his sport, leaping up to add more speed to his cane, and the strikes really hurt. To show my contempt for the injustice, I learned to do funny walks down the classroom aisle after suffering punishment to suggest that it was all so unnecessary.

10

EVOLUTION, SCHOOL AND BOY

I often pondered what the school was trying to become. It was obviously started as accommodation for homeless children by a wonderful man who devoted his whole life to it and achieved miracles in the process. In time it became a kind of hybrid: a home, a religious foundation, an institution, and an educational establishment, then becoming a semi-public school within its first half-century. Not allowing shoes to be worn by pupils would prove to be a mistake in the longer term, especially with regard to its aspirations to become a public school. Although it quite literally kept our feet on the ground, the rule reduced children to the status of paupers, not just in the eyes of the world but, for many, in their own estimation. I did not care a jot for that, but others did. However, many flourishing public schools began in the same way as KPG, and much later, after Indian independence in 1947, it moved rapidly to establish itself as a good public school, while maintaining the same percentage of free boarders. School fees escalated to cover the recruitment of fully professional teaching staff to replace the British and Commonwealth volunteers who lacked the required qualifications.

The religious aspect of Scottish Presbyterianism sometimes was so rigorous that it seemed nearer to Calvinism, where the rules prohibited activities such as dancing, and insisted on strict Sunday observances: morning and evening church services, Sunday school, regular visiting preachers or missionaries, and daily prayers and Bible readings after both breakfast and tea, with morning texts to memorise and regurgitate every evening.

Discipline and work schedules applied to both house and school lessons, with no excuses accepted to miss any scheduled activities like hockey, football, swimming, Cubs, Scouts, Cadets and Cadet drills and camps. Every scrap of food placed on plates had to be consumed (never a problem for me), and bed-wetting was publicly punished by making the offender stand for breakfast in the archway below the stairs.

I objected to the cross-country runs, which seemed so pointless. We were already running great distances every day just to get from place to place, so running across a field, going uphill and downhill round in circles three times was just daft. I once chose to sit it out but was compelled to run the route alone after being discovered sitting on a rocky outcrop overlooking the course.

Standing for Grace before eating and giving thanks following meals was fine, except the final thought in my head was When is the next meal? because I was always hungry. The food was really good, with glorious fresh bread from the school bakery, tasty butter made locally and great hefty soups at teatime that had simmered all day and tasted of meat juices fortified with fresh vegetables. Each table had a large tureen of it, but many boys described it as 'pig swill', so I often had three bowls with some extra slices of brown bread spurned by those who only liked white. These additional gifts were life-saving for a rapidly growing boy, but I could easily have managed double.

I believed I was big for my age until I met the other three platoons at Cadet camps. The St Paul's boys more than matched my stature and appetite, amazing me with the vast quantities they consumed, which exceeded anything I had ever seen. I gained weight at those camps and always felt stronger, fitter and revitalised on my return.

I was not much use as a footballer and cricket was too slow, but I found puddocks more enjoyable. The game was similar to rounders where players had to strike a ball with something similar to a baseball bat then run between wickets, but even that attracted only a limited attention span.

Some sports I liked. I enjoyed hockey and short sprints of 100 yards and 220 yards. Occasionally I attempted the quarter-mile, in which event I broke the junior school record simply by refusing to allow a boastful distance champion to beat me. It gave me great satisfaction, and astonished everyone else.

Being told as a 13-year-old that I was attempting high jump from the wrong direction and that my style was wrong, I then broke the junior high jump record (and never surpassed that height again because I couldn't be bothered to try).

In my penultimate year at school I entered every event in the annual swimming gala because no one had mentioned my name (quite correctly) as a contender for honours. Despite gaining a single point out of 40 for the diving events — awarded, according to H.T. Bamfield, simply for trying and not for any ability — I managed to accrue a greater overall points total in the pool than anyone else and became individual boys' swimming champion for 1943. No one could believe it, and couldn't understand why I opted out completely in 1944. Once again, I had no wish to prove anything.

St Andrew's was Number 4 platoon in the Cadets under the banner of NBMR, the Northern Bengal Mounted Rifles (such a romantic sounding name in those glorious days of Empire!). All the platoons came from schools in North Bengal, mainly in the district of Darjeeling. One was in Kurseong. St Paul's Cadets were Number 1 platoon and St Joseph's Number 2. Number 3 is lost in my memory, but they were all overseas off-shoots of British public schools built for the children of expatriates in the service of Empire. Ours was the only school with a pipe band, so during marches at camp where all platoons took part, the drums and pipes of St Andrew's always led the parades. They were so popular that they were asked to play at the evening campfires.

I began as a piper, but I was so bad that they quickly moved me to the bass drum. After damaging both drum skins during a wet route-march, I finally ended up as platoon sergeant where I enjoyed barking orders from a great distance.

Where there are Cadets, there are guns. We used old Lee-Enfield rifles which were 'mounted' on the shoulders. I always maintained that I did not deserve to be picked as a marksman to represent the platoon in the inter-schools Baker Shield shooting competition, where the best seven shots were chosen from each school. During the trial shootouts I could barely make out the four-feet square targets at both 100 and 200 yards, and was convinced that the boy next to me kept hitting my target by mistake, moving me into top spot. As usual, the team was soundly beaten by all the other platoons.

11

LEAP IN THE DARK

The time approached for a new beginning, and it was scary.

I took my final exams in an empty school, all the other pupils having departed for the long Christmas break, which created an unnatural, tomblike atmosphere in the building. I wrote the exams in the same trancelike state, not caring about what I knew or did not know, unconcerned about the results.

I would soon leave the school forever. Miss Coutts must have had a soft spot for her lone pupil because she produced a safari suit for me — jacket and matching long trousers fashioned from her favourite roll of grey material. The four large jacket pockets gave it a modern look, and the togs were the first ever 'longs' in my life. Worn with new shoes and socks, I looked quite presentable.

I sallied forth on 12th December 1944 armed with a small case holding a few books and little else to board the slow DHR train to Siliguri in the foothills of the Himalayas. From Siliguri I caught another train that would take me back across the great plain to Sealdah Station in Calcutta. Long before my arrival I realised with some trepidation that it would be night in the city when I alighted. I was worried, uncertain about what to do or how to do it, a young man who had never been alone in a city of any size during the 17 years of his life. On this return trip to the city I had last seen 10 years earlier, I remember crossing over the River Ganges, something that I did not recall seeing as a child.

Walking cautiously across the station concourse, pausing to look around several times, I headed towards the main exit when I felt a tap on my shoulder. I turned to see an Indian army captain in uniform who enquired politely in perfect English if I needed help.

I explained that Calcutta at night was not an inviting place for a country bumpkin like me.

The officer nodded, and said, 'Right, we will just have to wait for the dawn.'

He indicated two long benches joined at right angles where he suggested we could sleep. I was startled, but he smiled and pointed to his batman, a squat, burly figure.

'He will sleep on the floor between us and we will be fine.'

With that astonishing introduction to a big city, I felt completely calm and slept dreamlessly. I was woken early by my rescuer, offering me a mug of tea. We chatted for some time, the captain explaining that I reminded him of his own son who was a similar age.

'He is back at home in the village where we have our home and I will be seeing him again in three weeks,' he said, looking pleased.

Eager to help, he asked where I was going next. He knew the area of my destination: Birkmyre Hostel. Summoning a tonga, he told me exactly what fare I should pay for the trip, and then bade me farewell with a salute and a smile.

On arrival at the hostel, I paid the advised fare but the driver demanded more in a loud voice, which alerted someone from within who agreed that the payment was correct and saw him off. I was made welcome, given breakfast, time to relax and clean up before setting off again for Howrah Station to catch a train to Jubbulpore (now Jabalpore) in the Central Provinces — to see my mother.

While I had been at boarding school, she and my stepfather had to flee Burma following the Japanese invasion in 1942. They had caught the last plane out before the airport was bombed, taking only what they could each carry in one hand. They left behind their house, farm, and the successful delivery business they had built up over several years.

My mother had arranged with the school that I would stop for a brief visit to see her and my stepfather before moving on to Bombay. By the time I arrived at Howrah, the city heat had built up; it was humid, crowded and noisy, with strange odours issuing from the Hooghly River, all of which brought on a bad headache. I did not want to be there at all and just sat on my case in the middle of the concourse, head in my hands, becoming clammy with sweat.

Just about the time that I began feeling really ill, I heard a voice say, 'Hullo, it's Willie Cribb, isn't it?'

That Scottish version of my name was always used at school. I looked up to see a stranger. Too fuzzy-headed to think clearly, I stood up and followed him meekly into the station dining rooms, sat down at a table and waited patiently for him to return with a cup of tea and some tablets for my headache.

It was one of those times that tea and tablets worked so rapidly that I quickly became a different person and soon asked my new companion who he was. His name was not familiar because he had left KPG many years earlier, and had since become the dining halls manager at Calcutta's main train station. He never explained how he had identified me, but said that he had revisited the school several times since leaving. He asked where 'Willie' was going, told me that there was a long wait for the train, and invited me up to his flat at the top of the building overlooking the river.

'Have a shower, lie on the bed and sleep,' he said, 'and I will wake you in good time for the train.'

When I woke, I felt refreshed and ready for anything. As we set off for the platform I saw that my new friend was accompanied by an assistant carrying a large box filled with what he described as 'provisions for the long journey'. It had been prepared specially for me while I rested and would prove to be a life-enhancing bonus on the trip to Jubbulpore. Which guardian angel, I wondered, kept moving on ahead to help me on my way.

Jubbulpore lies around the halfway point between Calcutta and Bombay travelling east to west across India, a distance of over 1,000 miles by rail. My box of goodies had everything to sustain me on the long journey: sandwiches, fresh fruit, cakes, cold drinks and chocolate bars well-wrapped to stop them melting. There was enough to feed a young man with a good appetite, and made sure I arrived at Jubbulpore Station in good physical shape. But my hearty eating was accompanied by daydreams imagining my welcome, so I blanked out much of my travelling time. With an equal mixture of anticipation, anxiety, uncertainty and hope, I wondered how my mother would greet me after 10 years away, whether I would still feel uncomfortable with Conrad G., my stepfather, and how long I would be expected to stay with them.

I can recall a father and son sitting opposite in the carriage who chatted away happily, the son glancing at me occasionally and remarking about my red face, not in English but in Hindi, a language commonly spoken in northern India. Sometime later the boy said he needed the loo and they looked both ways for it.

I pointed, and said, 'It's up there.'

His dad smiled, and said, 'Thank you.'

Then the penny dropped.

'You understand Hindi,' he said.

When I nodded he blushed.

'Did we say anything to upset you?' he queried.

I smiled, shrugged, and replied that children always spoke their minds and I was not at all offended by anything he had said.

We travelled through miles of flat, open countryside bordered by small ramshackle dwellings dangerously close to the railway embankment, with lines of both males and females squatting and relieving themselves. The start of our journey westwards took us through two of the poorest states in India across the south of Bihar, cutting across the northwestern corner of Orissa, skirting the Central Provinces up to Bilaspur, and then heading north to Katni before the final short stage south to Jubbulpore. The names of those two states had been coupled to become Birissa, used as a name for a girls' cottage in Kalimpong.

Just when it seemed that the journey would be uneventful the train began slowing over a great distance, and then gradually braked to a complete stop. The scene outside was magnificent. We appeared to be approaching a huge sea. In front of the train there was nothing but water as far as the eye could see. But it wasn't the sea, it was flood water. We were sitting well above water level, but several hundred yards in front the embankment and waterlogged railway lines were just visible.

This was a new experience for me but everyone else seemed unconcerned.

A guard walked down the carriage, and said, 'It's all right, the waters will subside, we just wait.'

Asked if this was a common occurrence, he shrugged and said that it happened sometimes but not as badly. I found it difficult to believe that we would soon be moving, but incredibly our wait was much shorter than I expected and within an hour we were on the move again, tentatively and slowly at first, so the water can't have been very deep. Travellers in India never seemed to worry too much about time in those days just so long as they arrived at their destinations.

Following my arrival at Jubbulpore station my daydreams seemed to carry me to the gates of the Gun Carriage Factory, where my mother and stepfather lived. I can't recall how I managed to get there, but I remember not being surprised to see that the long, open staircase just within the great gates was identical to the picture magically conjured up in my mind.

The hoped-for figure of my mother standing at the top of the stairs to welcome her son with open arms proved to be a disappointing illusion. I got a tentative hug from her, which was somehow no more than I expected when I saw that my stepfather had precisely the same proprietorial attitude towards her that I remembered from early childhood. My feelings about him were precisely the same as 10 years earlier.

Their huge flat was set above and between the two great stone walls of the deep gateway to the right of the massive steel entrance gates. Below, an open area the size of a small football pitch extended into the factory. Barracks below the open balcony housed the military unit assigned to guard the main entrance and all the other gates in the factory walls.

A British colonel commanded the military personnel responsible for overseeing the production and testing of the artillery at the factory. Consequently, I could often hear firing in the distance. It was like a small town completely surrounded by high walls, although I saw no more than the main entrance and the flat.

My stepfather was in charge of the staff concerned with secure entry and exit duties, and also the telephone operators located between the double gates. The operators worked on switchboards of yesteryear: masses of retractable leads that were plugged in and pulled out criss-crossing a wall of sockets — hopefully connecting the right people with each other.

12

A SHORT STOP ON THE WAY

My stay in the flat at the Gun Carriage Factory lasted about two weeks, and included my first Christmas for ten years in the world outside school.

Apart from sleeping, I ensured that almost all my time was spent away from the flat, especially after an incident on the day following my arrival. My stepfather was having a shower and I did something that I had secretly ached to do for years. I put both arms around mother and held her gently for a minute. I could sense that she was not completely relaxed about it.

When she heard the latch on the bathroom door, she whispered quietly in my ear, 'Let me go please, he is still very jealous.'

I complied and stepped back. I realised that being exiled to school bore little comparison to her double predicament of being forced to send her child away and lifelong subjugation by a jealous husband. I felt so sad, but it was too late for a remedy.

The situation at home only encouraged me to explore the new city, so those days in Jubbulpore were packed with activity. Looking back, I am astonished how much I managed to fit into that short period of my life: a new place, new people, the cinema, and learning to ride a bicycle lent to me by a trusting Indian telephone operator.

'Take it, Mister William,' he said. 'I am here all day, so it is okay for you any day you want.'

But there was a surprise in store for both of us. He did not know that 'Mister William' had never ridden a bike in his life, and the boy was equally ignorant that his 'steed' had dangerously poor brakes.

Previous accidents and scrapes at school proved useful lessons in survival techniques that I needed during those days. I had entered a different kind of 'jungle', learning to ride the borrowed bike in busy traffic and meeting a much more dangerous species of animal than I had ever encountered in the woods. I fell off several times. Once, wobbling dangerously to avoid crashing into women carrying loads on their heads, I was forced to leave the road and collapsed beside a railway line.

Walking back one afternoon after watching a film at the cinema, I encountered a flock of sheep coming towards me and stood aside to let them pass. A ram broke free and suddenly charged at me, its head down with intent. I took off at speed hoping it would stop chasing, but not that ram, it just kept on and on after me and I was glad that I could run fast. I must have covered several hundred yards before it gave up. When I stopped running I felt exhilarated, amused and puzzled all at the same time. I remembered how I was always the fall guy at school and shrugged it off.

I managed to get the hang of staying upright on the bicycle and rode it confidently on open roads, until on one occasion I found myself careering too fast down a long hill. The brakes were even worse than I had thought, but I might have been all right if a lorry loaded with long wooden planks had not passed me travelling at an even greater speed. The load spread out like a fan towards the back and caught me a glancing blow in passing, sending me spinning off into an open field. My only concern was the cycle, but it seemed to have a charmed life.

By the time I got the knack of staying upright my 'fame' nearly got me killed. Cycling through town an unexpected shout of 'Hey! Cribb!' from across the road made me turn and lose control. I suddenly found myself lying under a horse-drawn tonga. The metal-rimmed wheel had run over my ankle and the bike lay beside me, now with twisted handlebars. Several people rushed to help me up. One said that I was lucky because a hoof that had just missed my head would have killed me. I asked someone to please straighten the handlebars and check that it was otherwise okay; he was amazed at my priorities. I never discovered who had called out my name but it could only have been another 'old boy' from Kalimpong. Perhaps he was reluctant to be identified as the one who almost got me killed.

With one leg dangling painfully, I cycled back, left the cycle at the gate and hopped upstairs. Mother wanted me to get medical attention, but I assured her that if it was bound up tight the leg would be fine. I said that it was comparatively minor compared to everything that had happened at school. It hurt a lot but I refused to let it show. The ankle took several months to heal properly.

Two days later I was back cycling using both legs, the good one doing most of the work, and I was careful to use open roads away from the busy town. The telephone operator seemed oblivious that his bike had suffered several spills and accidents. I never told him about them.

I made good use of my two days' recuperation by getting to know a sergeant in charge of the Rajput guard, a man who treated me with courtesy and repeated almost exactly what the captain at Sealdah Station had said.

'You remind me of my son who is about your age.'

His son was also miles away in their home village. He invited me to share a mutton curry, an invitation taken up several days later when I was introduced to some others in his platoon. There were separate Indian ranks such as Havildar (Sergeant), Naik (Corporal) and Lance Naik, Subedar and Jemadar — the last two, dropped since Independence, remain unexplained. Most of these names were changed at or after Partition in 1947. Enquiries about the ranks many years later, of a young Indian Army officer, drew a blank look.

During my short stay in the flat, I had a chance to be alone with my mother only once, helping her to mix a Christmas cake, but her state of mind failed to lift my spirits.

I remember her repeating, 'Never marry unless you are rich enough to support a wife because when there's no money, love flies out of the window.'

I often wondered what kind of life she had lived with my natural father and the closeness or otherwise of their relationship. I always suspected that his well-known generosity with both his time and money had left her almost destitute when he died so young and so unexpectedly.

13

THE NEXT STAGING POST

Early in January 1945, my mother bought another train ticket for me. I was to leave Jubbalpore and head for Bombay. What waited for me there, I knew not. I had the same indifference to my future plans as on arrival. I was unconcerned about what I would do when I got there because I now felt able to cope with whatever life threw at me. Parting from my mother allowed me to feel her great sorrow, which she was careful to conceal from her husband, knowing that we would be unlikely ever to meet again. That sorrow has always remained with me, deepening instead of diminishing as I grow older.

During my 10 years at boarding school I had never received a letter or telephone call from my sister Charlotte. Learning that she and her family were in Bombay, my next destination, was news to me. According to Mother, Charlotte had departed Burma long before the Japanese invasion, with what future intentions I never discovered. I was about to meet a sibling who had never been close to me, even as a child. Her main concern had always been with her own husband and children. It was something I had never thought about at any stage of my short life, having been preoccupied with the problems of my own development.

The train took me 600 miles southwest, 300 miles south of Jubbalpore. Most of the route lay between the Mahadeo Hills (Maha meaning great or palatial as in Maharajah and Taj Mahal) and the northwest boundaries of the Central Province. The train travelled via Bhusawal before crossing over the magnificent mountains of the Western Ghats at Thal Ghat. Many of the nine or more rivers we crossed ran north–south except for the Tapti River which continues its long journey westwards to join the sea at the Gulf of Cambay (now Khambhat) at Surat.

This range of mountains starts just below Surat, and acts as a barrier, creating a long, narrow strip dividing the west coast from the rest of the Indian land mass, and extends southwards into Kerala, becoming (then) the Sahyadri Mountains. I remember seeing mountains covered by tropical rainforests, which have since become a UNESCO World Heritage Site. The area was filled with a variety of wildlife ranging from creatures that scuttle or slither to flying insects, butterflies, birds and every size of animal up to the Indian elephant.

The train travelled slowly around tortuous bends on lines bridging high gorges with streams far below, many with narrow, open and perilous wooden crossings. We went through dark tunnels, past water cascading across the tracks, while staring out at incredible views of dense forests and peaks at every bend.

No other train journey had offered such sights as these, and despite being a dreamer I could not fail to marvel at the magnificence of the surroundings. A fellow traveller said that he crossed the Western Ghats often just to enjoy the journey after leaving his job with Indian Railways because, 'I was too busy working to enjoy looking around.'

I guessed that he had worked in a city office somewhere and not actually on the trains, and when pressed he suddenly opened up.

'Nagpur was a place I did not know,' he said, 'until I was posted there from Delhi, but the offer came along just when I was coping with a lot of stress in my personal life.'

It turned out that he had once been a senior employee but still managed to retire with a lifetime free train pass .

The man (who told me, 'My name really is Smith') got off at Kalyan, just before Bombay.

My sister and her eldest son Hector met me at the station, which provided my first surprise. My nephew looked so uncannily like the brother I had last seen 10 years earlier, that I felt I had stepped back in time. It is amazing how resemblances can pass down a generation through a close family member. However, my astonishment was quickly forgotten when my sister asked if I had any money. I handed over what cash I had in my pocket. She took it and immediately bought a bottle of rum for her husband, Sam, who was back at the house. She promised to pay the money back. She didn't. I was happy to forget about the outstanding loan, but two days later I learned about more serious problems she had with her husband.

Charlotte and Sam lived in Bandra, then a quiet retreat on the mainland sheltered from the hurly-burly of the city. In those days, moving further inland and away from Bandra Station, it was easy to find open and peaceful areas. Since the population explosion, in what is now called Mumbai, thousands have moved into these suburbs, which I'm certain has changed its character.

The following day, Sam asked me to accompany him by train into Bombay. What he wanted in the city never came to light, but after a short while he began behaving very strangely. He took out his wallet, keys and other personal items from his pockets and thrust them all at me, exhorting me to keep them away from him no matter what he said. We got off the train at the next station and took the next service back to Bandra. When we returned to the house, he dashed into his bedroom from where, moments later, I heard strange shouts. Then my sister emerged to tell me he was suffering from the DTs again, which was all new to me. She explained delirium tremens, and how it was the result of the long-term effects of alcoholism.

Peering into the bedroom, I could see him waving his arms, shouting and pointing to hallucinations, such as snakes or flying objects. That was my introduction to the problems connected with alcohol, and how it had been a lifelong headache for my sister.

Their son Hector was not my only nephew, there was also Conrad and niece Judy (whose real name was Elaine). I was surprised to see that they were all being educated at a local Roman Catholic school. My sister had converted for the sake of the children because she believed Sam was setting a poor example. It was her attempt to maintain some family unity. She enlisted aid from priests to help Sam overcome his addiction, but it didn't work and she had finally given up on that approach.

British-built electrified train services from Bandra into Churchgate Station, Bombay, were fast, efficient and ran at regular intervals. Mainline trains went as far as Victoria Terminus, another mile away.

I quickly found my way around the city, meeting and getting to know several people. One man in uniform said that he was based at COD (Central Ordnance Depot) Kandivili, a large military transit depot for SEAC, or South East Asia Command. When I said that I needed a job he told me that the O.O. Admin. Officer, second in command of the station, required an assistant. I made my way there immediately.

Earning an immediate income was important because I did not expect a free ride, especially after the revelation about my sister's financial problems. In complete ignorance of what I was about to do, I marched into the central ordnance depot and announced that I had come to see the major. I was directed to his office.

Major MacDonald was sturdily built, of average height with iron grey hair, approaching retirement, and looked at me with an inscrutable expression.

'What can I do for you laddie?' he asked, with a distinct Scottish brogue.

'I have been told that you need an assistant,' I replied. 'So I am here to help.'

'Well then, where is he?' was his rejoinder, looking around.

I pointed a finger at myself, respectfully stood erect, and said, 'It's me!'

With a slightly amused expression, he asked, 'How old are you?'

I replied promptly. 'Nearly eighteen, sir,' I said, trying hard to keep a straight face.

'Are you sure? You look about fifteen,' he said, which was true.

'But I am very capable sir,' I insisted, 'and can do whatever is needed.'

'Cheeky young puppy,' he said with a smile. 'But I need a CGO or a junior army officer to assist me. A lot of confidential information goes through this office.'

His smile encouraged me.

'The war is sure to end this year, sir,' I said, 'and in your position you can bend or even break the rules, and I am really very competent.'

'You really are a cheeky young pup,' his smile widening as he spoke. 'Come back tomorrow in uniform and start work.'

'Sir,' I said, 'I have been imprisoned for ten years so please don't make me await His Majesty's pleasure for release again.'

This time he did looked shocked until I explained my 'incarceration' at school. He then waved me away with a resigned look.

14

ARMY ORDERS

I arrived early for work that first morning in January 1945, and found Sub-Conductor RFG Fordham already there waiting for me. He had witnessed my interview with Major Mac (who I later learned was always so addressed) without comment, but now congratulated me for using a novel and amusing approach.

He explained that unusual designations like S/Cdr. or Conductor were only used in some army supply corps units. I regret never asking him (despite the 'sub') whether his two stripes equated to a corporal in other regiments. What really mattered was that he was quiet, intelligent, helpful and good to work alongside, and I guessed that in civvy street he would have been a valuable employee.

Later, Major Mac told me that as a regular army tank corps major he outranked the C.O. who, he said, was 'only' a war substantive colonel. It was my first lesson in how wartime rankings were viewed by long-serving regulars.

The Office of Administration consisted of four core personnel — the fourth being a handyman, often referred to as a 'boy' or 'runner'. Despite its size, this compact unit was the real power at COD Kandivli.

Next door to our office was a huge room with 80 or more clerks, typists and others (both civilian and military) who processed everything required by us quickly and efficiently. They were the true workhorses, linking administration to the entire depot of several thousand personnel.

My job was to do whatever Major Mac asked. A basic requirement was keeping Southern Army Orders up to date. Shelves were full of these regulations, with changes, deletions or amendments to them flowing in every day. At some earlier time during the war they may or may not have been important, but within a few weeks I began to wonder about their relevance. Someone in a place unknown to me was busy churning out masses of changes to existing orders, which required cutting, pasting, the removal of single words, lines or entire pages, or the addition of others, and so on and so on. I cannot remember anyone looking at these army orders, or if duplicates existed elsewhere in the depot. Who, I wondered, really understood what was happening in the real world outside those secluded offices. This would not be the last time that I had a strong sense of the gulf between the 'orders' coming down from above and life on the ground.

Some of my other duties were more interesting, including notifications of transfers in and out of the depot across all ranks and officers. The adjutant, Captain Malpass, soon made known his displeasure after my refusal to answer him on a confidential matter.

He told me, 'When I become C.O. in this place, I'll have your balls.'

My reply was a simple, 'Yes sir,' delivered with a straight face covering my instant dislike for him.

Colonel Ffoox, the C.O., did not approve of my appointment and would walk by with a disdainful look. A shortish man, he could have stepped straight out of the pages of Punch. His ample mid-section led the way, his chin always tilted up to retain the monocle over his right eye, and he always left the tiniest whiff of something behind as he sailed majestically past. He never spoke to me in all my time at the office, but I am certain that I heard him snort once.

Confidential matters never went beyond me, ever, but I opened mail addressed to Major Mac once or twice and read the contents before he snatched them from me, saying that they were just for him. When I countered that I was there to make his life easier, and most of what they contained was already in the newspapers, he said 'That is not relevant', but as he turned away I saw the smile he attempted to hide. He treated me like an errant son but knew that I would never discuss anything outside the office.

On one occasion, I saw two names on the incoming transfer list that looked familiar: Sgt. D. Robinson and Sgt. J.A. Robinson of the Women's Auxiliary Corps (India) — known as WACIs — and thought it must be a coincidence. But several days later, sisters Dorothy and Janet Robinson, ex-pupils from Birissa Cottage of St Andrew's School, arrived. We were all surprised to see each other because they were two of the only three girls from the same cottage (or any other cottage at school) that I had actually known before they were removed following their father's death around 1940.

An even greater coincidence was that their stepfather was the obnoxious adjutant.

I said, 'Sorry, but I don't like him.'

Dorothy just laughed, and said, 'We never liked him from the moment we met him, and can't understand how Mum can live with him.'

Thinking about my own situation, I realised that their mother may have been in a similar position to mine, and in need of financial security.

I was paid in cash, weekly, and was given a travel warrant for local trains plus an identity pass, which made travel cheap and easy. Additionally, someone passed on to me some other perks unavailable to civilians, mainly 'iron' rations (sealed, waterproof and long-lasting) that were normally only issued in the field of active service, which had escaped into our domain. Some were labelled as "K" rations; it was excellent stuff. I discovered later that they were standard issues to U.S. forces who deposited huge quantities when they were in a hurry to move on, then seemed content to 'forget' them. Strange things were happening in those times and wastage in the field was growing during the later phases of the war, especially in the U.S. sector.

Tales abounded of how American forces were supplied with luxuries denied to British servicemen and servicewomen, such as flying ice cream into Burma on special delivery. I was assured that these stories were true, and later heard other tales about the masses of equipment they left behind in Burma after the war because it was too expensive and inconvenient to remove.

While I was getting to know the job, I spent very little time at home. Even though the house was large enough, I did little more than use the bed to sleep. I gave my sister the majority of my income. She evidently needed it more.

15

PARTITION

Just beyond the midpoint of my stay in Bombay, the long history of British Rule in India ended with independence on 15th August 1947, and the partition of Pakistan. Bitter and bloody battles regularly took place before the official declaration, and it was impossible not to witness some scenes of violence and sense tensions between Hinduism and Islam.

Meeting some young people who lived on the eastern, or mainland, side of the wide causeway separating us from the city on Bombay Island, I was persuaded to join them at church one Sunday morning. They included a slightly older boy, Lou Creed, and his sister Hope who lived with their parents not far from us. I learned that the minister — Reverend Johnson — was responsible for all three churches in the diocese, and his manse was next door to Lou Creed's house. The Rev and his wife were to become even closer friends of mine. They had no children, but had wide experience of life in the business world. Padre Johnson had been a highly paid senior executive with an international company before opting to become a minister, giving up a chauffeur-driven car and a large residence in exchange for the big manse, low salary and no 'wheels'. Invitations for me to stay with both the Creeds and the Johnsons were never refused, and I was always made welcome.

I remember Mrs Johnson once admitting, sadly, that life had become difficult for her as a minister's wife, not just financially but also because she was expected by members of the congregation to act like an ex-officio minister herself. Before her new life, she did not understand the degree of involvement and long hours needed in her role — running meetings, knitting groups, organising and baking, listening to complaints about everything, and just how very tired she often became. I think her husband understood how she felt but he was one of those placid, patient men who plodded on regardless. When he was 'awarded' a small motorcycle to carry out his duties he was quite content. I witnessed this huge man (he was about 6' 5" tall and powerfully made) arrive through the gate astride this tiny machine and laughed out loud because it looked so ridiculous. He merely smiled and said that it was all the church could afford.

One Sunday at a church service I met a man called Tom Ashworth who was a longstanding friend of the padre. I can remember him leaning over the open bonnet of his car after a service. I said that he was in danger of getting oil on his suit, but he seemed unconcerned.

We had known each other for several months when Tom said, 'Come and work with me, William.'

I noted he had said 'with me' and not 'for me'.

With absolutely no idea of what he did for a living, I asked, 'What do you want me to do?'

'Come and see.'

We agreed to meet the following weekend.

The address to which Tom sent me was surrounded by high walls, which gave no clue as to what was contained within. He met me outside and we entered through two enormous, heavy doors. Inside the compound I could see a couple of multistorey industrial buildings with smaller ones dotted around, like a miniature township encircled by protective walls.

He explained what I was looking at. 'David Mills is part of E.D. Sassoon and Company, with mill number one over there.' Tom pointed to another building. 'That one is mill number two. The lower buildings are dye works, weaving sheds, engineering shops, rope-making areas, packing sheds and storage warehouses.'

He pointed again. 'That's the canteen.'

'All new to me,' I said, 'and I don't know anything about textiles. What do you want me to do?'

'Anything you want,' he replied.

I gave him a questioning look and he nodded. 'Whatever you want to do.'

I persevered, countering with another question. 'How do I fit into this place, and what is my role?'

'You would be a management trainee, have the same authority as other members of staff but directly answerable to your own manager, with all staff privileges like paid holidays and annual bonuses based on profitability. And before you ask, you can start in any area you wish: spinning, weaving or dyeing,' then added with a smile, 'or even in the engineering section.'

'How many others are there in the same position?' I queried.

'You will be the first, but we have another due to start soon, a protégé of the mill owner Sir Victor Sassoon. He's a multimillionaire racehorse owner with business interests in several countries. The other trainee will have the same privileges as you, but with added extras because he is due to marry the daughter of one of Sir Victor's oldest friends. I wanted to have someone like you with him so you could benefit from each other. He's currently a senior police officer and is due to give his notice at the appropriate time.'

'I, too, will have to give my notice,' I said, 'and I'm glad that, as a civilian, I'll be able to leave without awaiting His Majesty's pleasure.'

I would later learn just how important a position Tom Ashworth occupied. He was the Chief Executive Officer of all operations owned by Sir Victor Sassoon in Bombay.

We left it at that and when I returned to the COD I asked about my notice period. It should have been a month but a smiling RFG Fordham said that Major Mac would be flexible with me 'as always', and so I arranged to leave within a fortnight. They both said they were sorry to see me go and wished me well. The major added that he would soon be leaving for home, anyway, as his military service was coming to an end.

16

MAKING AN IMPACT

I left COD Kandivli sometime between V.E. Day in May 1945 and V.J. Day in August of that year. My sojourn at the depot had lasted less than six months, and now I looked forward to working at David Mills.

I had already decided that the best way to learn about textiles was to roll up my sleeves. I wanted to get involved in the production process and start from the very beginning, i.e. where the raw material entered the mill. This seemed a natural choice to me. It had not been long before this that I had been used to physical labour at school. I knew that work was done by people's hands. Why not carry on like that? I did not want to wander around, detached, and looking lost. I wanted to learn about textiles by doing, by getting enmeshed in the place. Although I could not understand its full implications at the time, I am very glad that I made this choice.

I approached the spinning master, the man in charge of both spinning mills. His workers were all locals, drawn from various sects, mainly Hindus. Most spoke or understood

English, but their first language was usually Hindi or Gujarati with a sprinkling of Punjabi and some southern Indian languages. Mr Saldana seemed surprised that I was prepared to work 'in the mill', but on my assurance that hard work would not be a problem, he said that I ought to speak to the supervisor of each department and get their agreement because no member of staff had ever volunteered to do this before.

Both the opening and carding machines and the speed frames occupied the entire bottom floor of the four-storey mill No. 1, the more modern mill of the two. I sought permission of the carder to work there under his guidance and asked him who was responsible. When I saw his reaction, I understood why Mr Saldana had suggested that route.

I smiled, and said, 'Give it a try and if you are unhappy then I will back off.'

He agreed, but only on condition that I first spend a week in the engineering department, 'To get used to textile machinery parts and identify which departments they come from.'

He was a wise man, and soon got someone else to check me out. I could see what he was doing, but made no comment and started work in the machine shop.

I was given a full tour. I was shown the lathes, milling, drilling and cutting machines, work benches, planing tables and machine parts awaiting repair, then given a piece of mild steel plus a cold chisel and asked to form a hexagon. The steel was clamped in a vice and after a demonstration of how to use the chisel I was left to get on with it. Great, I thought, this is easy. I kept going until I had one passable face of the hexagon, then released it from the vice, turned it and clamped it back in the vice to start the next face and carried on. It's amazing how quickly two or three hours can pass. I noticed that I was getting concerned glances from other workers and thought that I must be doing something wrong but couldn't understand what it could be.

By early evening my arms began to ache. By bedtime the pain was so unbearable that sleep was impossible. Realisation dawned that all those looks were expressions of concern for my wellbeing, but no one had wanted to stifle my enthusiasm. The next morning, several people asked how I was and expressed their admiration for the effort I had put in on my test piece. It was not brilliant, but the piece vaguely resembled what I had been asked to produce. Once filed and polished, it would have looked better, but as it had no practical use, I stopped work on it after filing one face. However, my efforts appeared to allay their fears about my ability to get on and graft, so during that first week I progressed to a few other basic chores in the machine shop under supervision. Before moving on, I was pleased to see that my hexagon had been glued end-on to a plaque, dated, and nailed to a wall.

Next was the blowing room, where I had to help feed and blend raw cotton and get to grips with the basics of opening, cleaning and forming 'laps', etc. A messenger handed me a book that illustrated the basic types of machinery required for the early processes in textile spinning and included a note saying that his technical library was always available to me whenever I needed to use it.

One week was sufficient in the opening room as I had no wish to become a weightlifter; the work was heavy, dirty and tiring, but I did my share of everything that needed to be done without shirking.

Next I moved into the card room. The first requirement was to check how the mill engine delivered power to the different departments and to follow it through to the overhead shafting, which drove all the machines. When I enquired how they knew that the line shaft speeds were correct, the other workers were amused and told me that it was on record. But I asked if I could check it as an exercise to satisfy my curiosity. They hooked up a ladder and gave me an instrument to measure the speed. When I called out the reading they told me to check it once more. The re-checked speed matched the first reading. Then the carder took a reading. He descended the ladder looking thoughtful. He said that I would have to report that all machine efficiencies were incorrectly based on the wrong line shaft speeds. The speeds were checked twice more on different days to be certain, but these confirmed the incorrect readings.

An engineer was called in to look at the mill engine and verify delivery speeds. He confirmed that everything was in order and agreed that our readings were correct. I offered to work on a daily basis with the team of fitters who cleaned, overhauled, and reset two carding engines a day. They checked that all gearing was as stated, and tested pulley and drive shaft diameters and everything else that needed inspection. Quite a few discrepancies were discovered and replacements made. Consequently, the new readings meant a new manual had to be written for both lines of cards that ran the length of the room.

Over the course of several months, I helped dismantle, clean and rebuild all those carding engines and became friends with the group of workers, sharing food and tea with them. They trusted me to use all their tools and feeler gauges, but I insisted that they double-checked all my settings because we worked on fine tolerances.

When bonuses were paid for that year (early in 1946), I was amazed to be awarded a full annual bonus for my few months' work late in 1945 for my contribution to the production of a new works manual. Tom said that he had not initiated the award, but had approved a submission by both spinning managers: Mr Saldana and Mr Bhatt. I gave my salary bonus to my sister. She was stunned but grateful, so I gave her my bonus every year I spent there.

17

COMPLETING THE PACKAGE

I made steady progress through the mill and my hands-on knowledge grew each day. By this stage I had been joined by Fred Stuart, protégé of the company chairman, and he agreed that we should both take the concentrated two-year academic spinning course. It meant spending Saturday mornings at the VJTI, or Victoria Jubilee Textile Institute, in the city.

Fred was at least 12 years my senior and we differed in two ways: he thought that I was a bit crazy to work my way through the mill; and he confessed that he would fail the course because he had a poor grasp of mathematics. I offered to teach him maths, starting from absolute basics as he would need the subject for almost everything we had to do at college. He agreed.

Every lunchtime we sat in a room at the top of a tower and began our maths tutorials. The speed at which he picked it up was incredible, soaking it up like a sponge, and he quickly advanced beyond the basics.

About the fourth week, Fred said, 'I wish you had been my maths teacher at school, everything seems so easy and fun when you explain it.'

Within a few months he had progressed enough to understand the rules for applied mechanics, enough to know how formulae were derived. I could feel his love for the subject expanding rapidly.

'When we finish our course,' he said, 'I intend to take up maths seriously because it is so interesting.'

For the record, he actually did so, going far beyond anything I ever did at school. In our second-year exams his high pass marks were just two behind mine and I would not have cared had they been higher. I really loved working with him.

Learning from each other was certainly a two-way process. He taught me about life from his experiences as a police officer and the realities on the streets of Bombay. He also introduced me to several serving police officers, contacts that would later prove to be very helpful.

During the summer of 1946 the tropical heat, humidity and heavy work I was doing began to affect my health. I lost my appetite and had trouble sleeping. I became skeletal and survived on fruit alone because I had no desire to eat anything substantial. I did not realise what was happening until Fred pointed out that I was fading away before his eyes.

'Adolf,' he said (I have no idea where he dug up his name for me), 'if you don't see a doctor you haven't much time left on earth.'

I did as Fred advised and saw a doctor, who agreed that I needed to eat more. He prescribed medication that I dutifully swallowed with no belief that it would work, but to my surprise it did and my appetite slowly returned. When the bottle was empty I read the label for the first time and was amused that, along with several other ingredients, it contained a very high level of alcohol. I regained most of my lost weight but never all of it. The important factor was that I certainly felt better. Nevertheless, realisation was slowly dawning that the heat and humidity of Bombay did not agree with me and that sooner or later I would have to leave for an English climate.

It took over two years for me to go through all the processes of cotton spinning, by which time I had dismantled, cleaned and re-erected all the machinery (except the spinning frames), and had produced a new manual for the slubbers, inters, and roving frames in No. 1 mill. By this time everyone on the shop floor treated me as a friend. A quiet man who seemed to be a general labourer or handyman was especially courteous and helpful although he said very little to me. He was big, powerfully made and well respected — mainly, I thought, because he ran a gymnasium to which many people seemed to subscribe. But there was more to this quiet man than met the eye.

Early one morning in 1947, on my way from the station to David Mills, I saw a man staggering towards me who seemed to be the worse for drink. But as he drew near I could see that his body was covered in stab wounds and his clothing soaked in blood. It was the quiet man from the shop floor.

He veered off to one side and collapsed onto the street. I automatically moved to help him but a hand on my shoulder steered me away.

A voice behind me said, 'Keep walking, don't get involved, he's already dead.'

The hand propelled me to the mill gate and into the grounds. It was then that I learned more about the big man at the mill. He had issued instructions to keep an eye on me because he said I was too trusting and innocent and could end up in real danger.

'Who is he?' I asked of my companion.

The man said, 'He is a powerful gang boss and he does own a gym but that is all I can say about him. He likes you but says that you don't see danger anywhere so we watch out for you.'

I became more aware that the city was in the midst of serious battles between the two main religious groups but I never felt really threatened at any time even when I witnessed several clashes or saw buildings burning, most often on my train journeys.

Most of the staff in the complex showed a great interest in me and wanted to know about my life, and I was invited out to wonderful meals at various restaurants. Mr S.K. Nayar, who hailed from south India, was the dyehouse manager and introduced me to a different kind of cuisine to the local variety. I was never allowed to pay for meals, every host insisting that I was doing them a favour by offering each of them something new in their lives. They almost had me believing them, they were so sincere.

Some of the best food I ever tasted was when sharing meals with Nahome Sion, one of the senior staff, who had food delivered like thousands of others, directly from home. It was an incredible network of 'tiffin carriers' run by specialist groups who had hundreds of men running across the city with flat trays balanced on their heads supporting several tall containers, each destined for a different person. The carriers always arrived with the food still hot.

Nahome was a Yehudi Jew, but despite our religious differences we became good friends, although we never met away from our workplace. The food sent from home was always enough for three people.

Once he said, 'You must help me to eat these enormous meals my family think I need. Look at me, they want me even fatter, but I can't cope. Please eat with me so we can both gorge ourselves and have an enjoyable chat as well.'

He said, 'Never talk about it because we are an orthodox family and they would be appalled at us sharing food together.' He shrugged. 'I don't care, as long they never find out there's no harm done.'

18

PREPARING FOR THE FINAL STAGE

Herschel Hesse proved to be one of a select few people who illuminated my life in the 15 months that I knew him. Over 60 years of age when we met (I was not yet 20), he was a superb violinist who practised every day, and exercised daily with dumbbells and Indian clubs. We took long walks together along the coast in the evenings. With short, red-gold hair around a balding head, a powerful neck, shoulders, wrists and arms, he looked (and was) a very strong and fit man with a Teutonic countenance. It was difficult to believe that following a three-month trek from Burma to escape the Japanese invasion, he had finished like a skeleton in a Calcutta hospital. He told me of his determination to regain his health so that he could indulge his lifelong love affair with the violin. As a young man he had appeared on the same stage as the sopranos Dame Adelina Patti and Amelita Galli-Curci.

His experiences in life were of benefit to me, and it was Herschel who advised me to 'go home' because, he said, 'Hot tropical conditions are not for you, nor is anything else here, so go whenever you are ready.'

He brought home to me the importance of maintaining physical fitness by exercising all parts of the body (including eye exercises that he demonstrated) and deep breathing. He also said that strength and fitness were vital for a serious musician to make any instrument sound good.

He was right about the effect of heat and humidity on me, especially in the build-up to the monsoon season. There were times when I felt so ill that death would have been a release. But when the deluge came, we would stand outside wearing nothing but briefs and allow the rain to soothe our prickly heat. One evening we were sitting outside waiting hopefully for rain when we saw a bandicoot, a marsupial that looks like a large rat. It emerged from beneath a bridge over a culvert, or open storm drain, designed to cope with monsoon rains. It proved to be the only bandicoot I ever saw. I even wrote a poem about it to express my awe.

In 1948, a lovely, fair young girl called Eileen Lightfoot, on holiday from southern England, said that she was able to tolerate as much sunshine as she liked and ignored our warnings about the dangers of too much sun. Unfortunately she got heatstroke and died a week after arrival. Everyone who had known her was very shocked and distressed.

Another lady remained in Bandra for three or four years after the death of her husband because, she said, 'What will our servants do if I leave them now? They have been with us for many years.'

Even though she employed a cook, a gardener and a houseboy, she did almost half the work herself — 'So that I don't get out of the habit when I go home.'

She was a decent, quiet, middle-aged woman from Lancashire. So decent was she that she offered me a gift of either the American car or the British saloon in her garage. Apparently one was surplus. I declined the offer without seeing either of them, thanking her and telling her that I did not need a car.

I wrote a letter to the Kalimpong school superintendent, James Purdie — known as P.B. — and told him of my plans to leave Bombay for England. I was amazed to receive an immediate reply informing me that Thomas Cook had instructions to give me passage on any vessel when I was ready, and that the journey had been paid in full. There was no mention of whether it was a gift or a loan, just a simple statement of fact. To say that I was astonished is an understatement. I made a mental note that whatever it cost would be repaid in full, with interest. Years later I made good that promise.

With a lifetime to think back on those times, I realise now that so many 'coincidences' had P.B. behind them. I now think I have worked out why he kept an eye on my progress. He was an intelligent and observant man who missed nothing that happened at school. I recall his invitation to tea, twice, in 1944 when he seemed concerned about my final three years because St Andrew's had not been able to provide teaching to Senior Cambridge level at the time, although he had covered it by asking innocuous questions. Even at a young age I was able to pick up what lay behind such questioning.

With the invitation to England in my pocket, I visited Thomas Cook in the city and they confirmed what I had been told.

The clerk said, 'Tell us when you are ready to leave and we will get you to Tilbury on the next ship.'

Something that had never crossed my mind before, and another shock for me, was that I had no passport and could not remember if I had ever seen one on my transfer from Burma to India as a child. But this apparent obstacle was cleared by an unseen hand. I filled in the appropriate forms, signed the passport photos, and visited the passport control office in Bombay.

I was pleased to see George Barrow at the office, a senior police officer I had met once or twice.

He said, 'Hello William, what can I do for you? Ah! You want a passport. You're in luck, the Commissioner is in today and I'll get the forms signed right away.'

And sure enough he returned with the forms approved and signed in a few minutes, saving me a wait of three or four weeks.

He said, 'Take them across the road to the passport office. When you call back to pick up your passport they will be unable to find it, and will wait to see if you offer a payment, a standard method they adopt. Just play dumb and say that you will refer back to me to complain that there must be something wrong.'

He was absolutely right; it played out exactly as predicted. When I offered to refer back to George the man said, 'Hold on and we will look again.'

My passport appeared within minutes accompanied by apologies.

When I spoke to Tom Ashworth about my return to England, he asked if I had clothing suitable for a colder climate, another consideration to which I had not given any thought. Tom offered me one of his new suits, which had been tailor-made at Whiteaway Laidlaw. The suit could almost have been made for me, and was my first ever suit by a bespoke tailor. Tom insisted that it gave him pleasure to see me in it and wished me a good journey, and handed me a letter addressed to his brother Walter in London that I was to deliver in person. He asked where I was staying on arrival and I was able to tell him that I had become friends with a Captain C.L. George (by then retired to Essex) who had invited me to live with his wife and family as long as I wished.

My passage from Bombay to Tilbury was booked on the s.s. Chitral. As I recall, we sailed on 25th June 1949. My sister came to the dockside, wept, held me tight, and apologised for taking everything from me and leaving me with nothing. I was unable to console her, even when I said that I would have given all the money away wherever I had stayed, but was pleased it went to her.

19

'IT WAS LATE JUNE'

The title of this chapter is borrowed from the first verse of Adlestrop by Edward Thomas, one of my favourite poems that expresses, very simply, so much about the feeling of being in England. June was also the month when I set out to fulfil my childhood dream of completing that hundred-year family circle started by my great-grandfather.

The s.s. Chitral was an old vessel that may have been converted back from a wartime troop ship. It was just about the right size — not too small and certainly not large, with a top speed of 15 knots. The best thing about it was the deck that ran all the way round the ship, which made it great for walking. My cabin had three bunks intended for six people, with just five occupied: two by the MacDonald brothers, William and Henry, returning to Dundee from the jute industry in the Sunderbans, Bill Douglas, another Scot travelling with them, George Thornton, and me. Still only 21, I was the youngest, and my companions took great care of me.

Their care began before I had acquired my sea legs, almost before losing sight of land, much to the amusement of all aboard. That first night all I heard was, 'You poor thing,' and 'Have you never sailed before?' and 'Here, take these pills.' I got more help than I could stand. By dawn I was fine and ready for anything, especially food.

Designed simply for travel from point A to point B, the ship was like a three-week luxury voyage to me because it gave me the freedom to just be myself, breathe fresh air, eat as much as I wanted, and walk around the deck looking out at the expanse of water. With each passing day I felt fitter and stronger, as if I was becoming a new man. The sea voyage stands out as perhaps the most interesting journey of my life: new experiences, new places, and an endless supply of wonderful food all combining with a desire to fulfil my longtime dream of a life in England.

It may have been on day two while I was walking the deck that I noticed a lady watching me from her deckchair every time I passed. Eventually she beckoned and invited me to sit beside her.

I was puzzled by her gaze, and then she asked, 'Is your name Cribb?'

'Yes.'

'Are you the son of Thomas and Ethel Cribb?'

Again I confirmed that she was right.

'Have you a brother Tom and a sister Ethel Charlotte?'

'Yes.'

There was a very long pause before she said, 'I didn't even know you had been born. I have never seen or heard from them for over twenty-five years, so you can't be over eighteen.'

I was in no position to argue because what she was saying was so incomprehensible. I waited for an explanation. It came after another long pause.

'You walk exactly like your father but look like your mother, unmistakably a Cribb because I knew them so well for many years.'

It seemed that I was unable to go anywhere without being recognised, even by people I had never met before. It was to happen again in the next few years, and the significance of the date we set sail would return to me once more.

After that encounter I cannot recall meeting the lady again. She may have retired to her cabin, or perhaps I was too busy enjoying myself. By this time I had been 'recruited' by an Anglican nun to help look after some orphaned children on board. She was the most delightful, bubbly and outgoing person, and totally irresistible. I just could not refuse to help her, and in so doing I found it fun and enjoyable.

The children were five Desbruslais sisters who had been raised by the eldest two, Jean and Pam, after losing both parents. They were all involved as helpers together with the Rev. Fred Cromey and a few others. Many hands make light work, and it was not a chore. I had helped Fred and his wife carry aboard their very young child who sadly died during the sailing and had a burial at sea. I think the child's death may have been expected, although nothing was ever explained.

The ship's concert should have been fun, but my cabinmates had heard me 'playing' a mouth organ and put my name forward as an act. I could hardly refuse but my repertoire was amateur and limited in scope, so I got through it quickly and scuttled off the stage.

We went ashore at Aden prior to entering the Red Sea and again at Port Said after negotiating the Suez Canal before sailing through the Mediterranean. Part of our journey through the canal took place at night but we stayed up, not wishing to miss anything in case we would never sail through it again. I never have.

My new friends and I spent a whole day getting lost in Marseilles in southern France, our enquiries in schoolboy French eliciting blank looks from the locals when we asked our way back to the quay. The locals in port gave the impression that they were constantly quarrelling, with raised voices and arms waving about, but it seemed they were merely having normal everyday discussions — so very un-English. In desperation, I simply walked up to the next person I saw and asked, in English, how to get back to Cap Janet. To my surprise the man replied politely in perfect English (because he was English) and saved us from missing the boat.

The final part of the journey, crossing the Bay of Biscay, knocked over most passengers and half the crew when we ran into force nine gales. But now that I had my sea legs, I actually revelled in it, enjoying the sight of the huge waves, the roar of the wind and feeling of the ship being tossed about. I felt strong and indestructible, but looking across the expanse of water I realised that we are all so puny and helpless when nature lets rip. Inside, during mealtimes, as the ship pitched and rolled, I clutched at my sliding plates, eating everything served by stewards astonished at the quantities I consumed. During that three-week voyage I gained at least 20lbs and felt better and stronger than I had ever been in my life. All I had ever needed was lots and lots of glorious food placed before me.

They say the White Cliffs of Dover never actually had bluebirds over them, but as they hove into view everyone still standing gave a little cheer. The final stage up the Thames to Tilbury made me think of my great-grandfather setting out from the same spot just over 100 years earlier. It seemed that so many interruptions had delayed his great-grandson from completing the circle back to Tilbury.

20

LONDON

When the ship docked at Tilbury, I struggled with my case despite its small size because it was half-full of books; one, The Boy's Own Annual, Vol. 51, 1928-1929, weighed as much as a brick. An observant customs officer wanted to see what I was lugging about and registered amusement when he saw that there was little of real value, and wished me well on my travels.

With currency restrictions still in force, my passport registered that I had left India with £10 in travellers' cheques and some cash in sterling, but on arrival there remained just over £5, now all in cash. Instead of being sensible like everyone else, I did not join the boat train into London but took a taxi all the way to Pilgrims Hatch in Essex, which depleted my wealth by almost £3. This was the address I had for Captain Cyril George (retired). No one told me I would be met on the arrival of the boat train in London, nor did I expect to be, but then discovered Cyril George had gone to the city to await its arrival. Fortunately he was one of those unflappable, phlegmatic men who took everything calmly and shrugged off whatever life offered. I just wished he had let me know. His patient wife said that if he was sitting down and a herd of elephants careered through the room he would barely notice them, and I wondered how he had managed as captain in the army.

The Georges had three children: two boys and one girl, Audrey, who was asked by her mother to show me around Pilgrims Hatch.

She looked up and down at my unfashionable, off-beat clothing, and said, 'I'll wait till its dark.'

That amused me. Audrey may have been about 19 and very fashion conscious, so my defence mechanism of looking dishevelled to put off predatory females obviously worked.

The following morning I was up at six, walking along the hedgerows, breathing in the morning air and exulting in the soft Essex countryside, glad to be alive, and rejoicing in the fulfilment of my dreams. Always a romantic — in the broadest sense — I recalled lines from Rupert Brooke's The Soldier: "Gives somewhere back the thoughts by England given".

I took an early morning walk every day I stayed at Pilgrims Hatch, and always returned to a still sleeping household.

My training at school had taught me to do all the cleaning at my 'digs'. Mrs George said that I could stay there forever without charge. 'You're more useful than all my children put together,' she said.

It seemed to me, even at this early stage, that this could create discord in the family, so I reminded myself that the digs were only temporary. At the first chance, I would find my own place.

On the third day I travelled to London on a Green Line bus to deliver the letter from Tom Ashworth to his brother. With a quick glance at just two words on the envelope "Royal Arsenal", I found myself before the gates of the great armaments manufacturing plant in Woolwich. With great amusement, the sentry on duty pointed out that where I ought to be was at the Royal Arsenal Cooperative Society across the Thames!

I eventually found the correct address, but I was politely told that an appointment was needed to see Walter Ashworth, and refused admission. But I persisted, insisting that my letter for him had to be delivered in person. Walter finally arrived, apologised for his 'overprotective staff' and ushered me into his office upstairs. The sumptuously furnished room had a large table in the middle with a vase of flowers and a bowl of fruit on it, two comfortable armchairs, a big settee, and still had ample space for a huge desk.

'My word,' I said, innocently, 'you are well cared for at work.'

His modest reply was, 'Yes, they spoil me here.'

He called for tea and cakes. The girl who brought in the tray looked at me curiously, and I sensed that she was puzzled by my appearance as I still wore clothes that ought to have been discarded long ago. It began to register that perhaps I had missed something, so I asked Walter Ashworth exactly what his role was in the company.

'I was fortunate in being appointed managing director, which is an honour for a lad from Blackburn.'

I said, 'Two brothers from Blackburn each end up as chief executives of two separate organisations. It is an honour for me to have been associated with both.'

Like a practical North-countryman, he asked, 'Are you all right for cash?'

'Oh, yes.'

But he persisted. 'How much money do you have?'

'Enough,' I said.

He ignored my answer and handed me a £5 note.

Before I could protest, he said, 'That's from my brother Tom, not from me.'

I agreed to accept it as a loan and promised that it would be repaid as soon as I began work.

'You can come and work here with me,' he said, 'in this office, for two years, and when we open the new branch you can take charge of it.'

I was stunned by his offer.

'How do you know I will be all right to do that?' I asked.

'Because my brother said you can do anything. He has complete confidence in your ability and I trust his judgement.'

'I am really grateful for the offer,' I replied, 'but there's one minor problem. I can't see myself living in London indefinitely. It's too big, too busy, and too scary for a country bumpkin like me. I'm really sorry, but thank you very much just the same.'

He smiled and shook his head. 'Tom said you are always honest and direct. Let's try something else.'

He picked up the phone and called the manager of the local Labour Exchange. He told the manager that a friend would be coming to see him about a job and would he fix him up with whatever he wanted.

Before I left, Walter gave me his address at Crathie Road, Lee, in southeast London, and asked me to visit him at home.

As I made for the door, he said, 'Don't be so open with whoever you see about a job by telling them that London is only a stopgap. Just say that you need work.'

I went directly to the Labour Exchange and was ushered into the manager's office. He produced a few cards with company names on them, asking me to choose, so I picked up the one on top without even looking at it, thanked him for his help and returned home.

The name on the card read "Pantries Ltd", and the address was "The Minories", near Tower Hill, which I now planned to visit first thing the following morning.

21

PANTRIES

Next morning I caught an early Green Line bus from Brentwood to London, made my way to the office of Pantries Ltd and waited outside for the first arrival, who opened up the office and let me in. The man gave me a seat in the waiting room, but when the staff began trickling in between half-past nine and ten o'clock I realised that they were all wearing sober business attire. Some of the men wore bowler hats and I was still in my tatty old sports jacket and trousers. Their glances at me were polite but curious, obviously intrigued by this strangely dressed young man.

Apart from saying that Mr Oswald would see me presently, I was left to sit in silence. Mr Oswald was the company secretary and duly invited me into his office where we faced each other across his desk. He asked me very politely about my qualifications for the job.

I said, 'I have no idea what kind of person you want because I know nothing about the actual job to be done.'

Leaning back in his chair, he looked at me silently for a while, then said, 'We need an accountant.'

I replied, 'I know nothing about account books but should have no problem doing what is required if I'm shown the system being used.'

After another long pause, he placed a pad and pen before me, and asked for a brief outline of my life including exam results, perhaps checking to see if I was literate. While I scribbled away at speed he disappeared down the corridor. After 10 minutes he returned and read that I had sat for my senior Cambridge exams in 1944 at the age of 17, worked with SEAC in a responsible position, and with Sir Victor Sassoon (who I later discovered was known to his principals). I believe he was most relieved to see that I was articulate and able to write quickly and legibly.

He cleared his throat and announced, 'The principals of the company have authorised me to offer you a two-month trial at a salary of £5 a week. Personally, I cannot understand their reason for the offer.'

I thanked him, but said apologetically, 'Do you think, Mister Oswald, that £5 will be enough to survive in London? I honestly don't know anything about what it's like to live in this place.'

It was more of an innocent query than a request for more, but he sighed, shook his head sadly and left the room once again without a word.

Minutes later he returned, repeated that he still did not know why, but had been advised to offer £5 10s.

I began work the following morning.

I was soon brought up to speed about the company. I discovered that it was founded, owned and managed by Mr and Mrs Sibley, who must have walked past me when I was in the waiting room before my interview. The company ran between 30 and 40 cafés in and around London (and, oddly, an isolated one in Morecambe, Lancashire). They were all supplied by a fleet of delivery vehicles from their own bakeries. It was hugely successful, propelled by the energy and dynamism of its husband and wife team, but also by their sharp business accounting, which meant that head office staff were under orders to pay suppliers only when they became desperate. Consequently, they often took a lot of flak from irate creditors, but that was how the Sibleys had built their business from a single café: The Pantry.

Despite the excitement of starting work in London, my first working day proved unusual because few things I ever did in life proceeded without me dropping the odd clanger. At lunchtime I bought a large cox's orange pippin from a street vendor on London Bridge, then hopped on a bus to familiarise myself with the surrounding area, thinking that I would ride around for 20 minutes and catch another bus back to work. Alas for my neat little plan. I must have climbed aboard the wrong return bus, and found myself miles from my intended destination. I returned at least 80 minutes late, but I was pleased to see that my explanation was greeted with smiles and genuine pleasure at seeing me again. My bosses were worried that half a day with them had been enough! It seemed to me that the people at head office had already adopted this strange young man — and proved it in various ways over the next few weeks.

My job involved following the old bookkeeping system of debits and credits, in pounds, shillings and pence. The job was generally so easy that I could manage to do it neatly and accurately while chatting to others. The more difficult bit was deciphering some of the illegible scrawl on the weekly worksheets sent in from the branches, which sometimes required a telephone call to clarify figures.

There were 10 of us at head office, six males and four females, including Mr and Mrs Sibley. The only other director was Mr Hessy, a Bradford rugby league-supporting Yorkshireman who was a breath of fresh air, and brought northern directness with a great sense of fun to the place. He must have been very capable to have been appointed as the only other director because the principals demanded a lot from everyone. Keith Nightingale, the Sibleys' nephew, was quiet, friendly and helpful. David Fairbrother (who answered to 'Fairy') was big and powerful yet he was a gentle man; he moved and spoke slowly and could have been useful as an enforcer by his mere presence. Marie, secretary to the Yorkshireman, would often be found wrestling in the office with her boss to the disapproval of Mr Oswald, a very proper man, whose own secretary was Norah Morris. Last but not least there was Beryl Snazel, whose role was to look after the Sibleys. I adored her. She had an attractive personality, short fair hair, was young and beautiful — and knew that I was smitten. She was lovely in every way, not just a very efficient secretary. She did everything to make my life agreeable, but constantly teased me and blew me kisses. I warned her to behave or risk being smacked, so she leaned over inviting me to do so, which I did, very gently tapping her bottom.

She straightened up with the hint of a tear in her eye, and said, 'I thought you loved me, William.'

I said, 'I always will.'

She waltzed away and blew me a kiss, continuing as before, knowing that I thrived on it.

The Sibleys were not seen very much in the main offices, but on a rare visit by Mrs Sibley I noticed the simplicity of her appearance. A striking woman with dark hair casually gathered up on her head and held there with hairpins gave the impression that she had little time for trivialities, yet she looked beautiful.

My daily commute by bus to and from London was tiring and time consuming, so I enquired about accommodation closer to work. I soon found a room at 52-54 Mount Pleasant, a hostel described as a temporary residence for people seeking a permanent home London.

I took my minimal possessions from my digs with the Georges in Essex and moved into a small, basic room in the men-only hostel. It suited my needs: it was 20 minutes' walk from work — and it was cheap. Rather than treat tenants as strictly temporary, I soon discovered that no one appeared to mind however long you stayed. Yes, there were rules, like locking the front door at midnight, but helpful staff left a fire escape door unlocked at first floor level for those able to climb over the outer wall for late-night arrivals.

There were four huge, shared bathrooms downstairs, outside which were two great clothes racks that could be raised and lowered to dry washing. Best of all were the substantial breakfasts and evening meals that were provided by the all-female staff who ensured I always had enough to keep me happy.

22

52–54 MOUNT PLEASANT

Travelling from Mount Pleasant to work was easy no matter which option I took: I could walk, take a bus or the Tube. The 18b bus got me to the Monument for 2½d (tuppence ha'penny) in about six minutes. Following a quick walk down Grays Inn Road I could take a short tube ride from Chancery Lane to London Bridge, or just continue my walk via Holborn, Newgate, past St Paul's Cathedral and down Cheapside to the Monument. Whichever route I took, it was so much easier and quicker than the bus journey from Brentwood.

Walking past the long-gone Gamages department store one fine morning, I saw some demob suits on sale in the window. Acting on instinct, I went in and bought a really awful herringbone suit and wore it to work. Everyone was horrified at what the loveable and harmless eccentric had done, saying that the suit was as bad as the cheap, light flannel suit I often wore to the office.

Once I had saved £5, I called to see Walter Ashworth at home to repay him for his loan. He refused to accept it, and said that his brother Tom had already taken responsibility for the advance. I could not convince him to take it.

'The day will come,' he said, 'when you will be able to do the same for someone else and in that way repay Tom.'

As he predicted, that has happened several times since.

Walter also gave me an expensive Crombie overcoat. He said he had two. But though I used it once or twice it was too heavy and warm for this hot-blooded young recipient. One freezing cold evening I left Walter's house later than intended. I was wearing the coat but took it off and slung it over my shoulder like a sack when crossing the Thames so that I could run easier. A policeman stopped me and asked what I was running with, so I shook it out for him. I got an odd look in return because it really was a very cold and frosty night. He moved on and I rushed off for my bus.

Liaising with managers of the Pantries branches by phone to sort out problems was an enjoyable part of my job. One in particular I had to contact every week was a Miss Jones because her paperwork was impossible to decipher. It was suggested that I ought to visit her café and sort it out. I duly arrived and was met at the door by a gorgeous blonde: Miss Jones. The visit was a revelation for another reason. The café was well run by an all-female staff who liked and respected her as a practical and hard working manager. I made a note that in the circumstances her untidy paperwork was irrelevant. When I returned to head office they all awaited my reaction with interest, and much amusement.

The most memorable birthday of my life was at Pantries, a celebration with drinks laid on exclusively for this odd stray they had adopted and taken to their hearts. I was touched by their genuine care and concern and tried unsuccessfully to hold back a tear because no one had ever shown so much consideration before. I will always remember that 22nd birthday with fondness and gratitude, especially as it was my first on English soil. Mr Hessy's secretary Marie, though young and strong, was unable to drink even the smallest quantity of alcohol without becoming giggly, and sat over her typewriter the rest of the day producing utter gibberish, to the amusement of all.

When Mr Hessy acquired a new Bentley, he took all three men from the office to visit some of the oldest Shakespearian pubs in London. As an inexperienced imbiber, I had problems crossing the car park after the third hostelry. The ground refused to stop moving and I needed help to the car and to get home.

At the end of the year, the Sibleys' nephew, Keith, invited me to spend two nights over Christmas with the family at Gants Hill in Essex. They lived in a very large old house owned by another uncle and aunt, with a huge entrance hall facing an elevated landing across the back accessed by two staircases. All the rooms were in the same grand proportions. The Christmas tree must have been at least 12 feet high and sat comfortably under the high ceiling.

Charming and completely natural, everyone was left to introduce each other, and I was treated like a member of the family. I was even handed a broom at one point and asked to tidy up under the tree. I loved that welcome and felt at home instantly.

I was woken on Christmas morning by screams of laughter and saw a young couple still in their nightwear chasing each other across the landing, which set the tone for the whole stay. The tree was loaded with little presents for everyone, each one beautifully wrapped and labelled. I had several, some edible and some to keep. I still have a comb in a case from that wonderful first Christmas in England, another memory to cherish with joy.

Back in the real world, life at the hostel proved to be no less interesting, powered by the mixed bunch we had there: a few students, a courier, a budding artist, a jobbing actor, the identical Gibbs twins that I could never tell apart, Jimmy Thompson, a Scot from Dundee and another from Perth, two blind men — one polite and courteous; the other rude and demanding — and Mr Cannon, who decided to take me to the opera. He had once played second violin in an orchestra and with his friend, another opera buff, would act out both music and story for me as we walked about freely beyond the highest seats at the rear, which suited me well.

It was established custom at the hostel that some residents accompanied our off-duty female staff round some of the London pubs on one or two evenings. I joined the group sometimes. We would begin at the bottom of Grays Inn Road by calling at Wards Irish House (long gone) and then continue in a long circular walk from pub to pub ending at Kings Cross Station at about midnight, where we always had a full meal. Looking back, the quantities of food I consumed must have been prodigious because our evening meals at the hostel were always large. One evening at the station I had two meals.

I never drank anything stronger than lemonade or fruit juice, but some others liked a drink and often needed help to get home. One evening we helped a fellow tenant over the wall and wondered why it was followed by complete silence. On investigation we discovered him folded up, legs and feet in the air with his bottom jammed fast in a dustbin. He was out cold. It looked hilarious but we had to stifle our laughter and tip the bin on its side to pull him out. He reeked of rotten vegetables, so we dragged him up the fire escape and dumped him fully clad into the bath, finally stripping, drying him and putting him to bed. At no stage did he offer the slightest protest.

Those were happy carefree days and many of the 'inmates' were decent hardworking folk or students setting out on new careers. We shared many adventures, including one when I foolishly accepted a bet from the courier. I had agreed to match him drink for drink, and despite feeling awful halfway through, I refused to give in. Eventually I had to drag him home along Grays Inn Road and dump him on his bed. That was the worst night of my life during which I had to get rid of everything inside me once or twice, then sleep for three hours, have a bath and nonchalantly walk in for breakfast. Somehow he also made it down for breakfast. He kept looking at me and shaking his head.

'How can an innocent-looking youngster swallow all that booze and look so fresh in the morning?' he said.

Damned if I would ever let on how bad I felt after he had challenged me.

Another inmate, Basil A. Nubel, was the resident budding artist. When he found new digs, I helped him move out to a place at Kew, where he was to share an enormous hall with several others, apparently all kipping on the floor at one end and using the other end to paint.

23

NEW BEARINGS

Just before Christmas 1949, what had begun as an amusing incident at work became a serious consideration for me. One day I passed too close to the desk of Norah Morris, secretary to Mr Oswald, and my trousers snagged on the corner of her desk, ripping open all my fly buttons (no zips at the time). My trousers dropped around my ankles, which amused everyone. But practical Norah immediately summoned Keith to escort me to the lavatory and bring back my trousers so that she could sew up the buttonholes properly, which she did.

I had not had much contact with Norah before that, but always liked her very much as a person. Naturally — with my trousers repaired — I returned to thank her and chatted with her more from time to time in quieter moments. She was considerate, kind, capable and helpful, and we became quite friendly in what I imagined was a brother and older sister relationship.

Her boss came in one day and remarked that we should get married so we could have lots of time to chat. I laughed at his comment, which was not said unkindly. Looking at Norah, I saw her nodding a 'yes, yes,' and realised that she was in complete agreement with his suggestion. My immediate thought was This can't be happening, all my planning to avoid marriage is not working, there's someone here who does not care whether I have anything to offer because she already has substance of her own, so panic!'

I did not register real alarm until everyone else made comments like 'Norah is a fantastic person,' and 'She thinks the world of you,' and 'She is a good cook, has a big house left to her by her parents,' and so on and so on. Everyone in the place kept on about how wonderful it would be if we got married. By that stage I was becoming really concerned that I was sleepwalking into something I did not want. Yes, I liked her very much as a friend and could see her as one for the long term, but for a 22-year-old 'boy' (in life terms) she seemed so much older at 29, not that age would have really mattered to me. I never liked to be rushed into anything, and settling down in marriage, at any time, was not for me.

Then something unexpected — and well-timed — came up. Walter Ashworth had a friend in Lancashire who had a vacancy in his company that might interest me if I still wanted to leave noisy, boisterous London. Now, with Norah breathing down my neck, I had an additional reason to move. I contacted his friend, Arthur Duckett Of Joshua Hoyle and Co. at Bacup, to arrange an appointment.

One cold winter Saturday I caught the train to Manchester, then took a bus to Rawtenstall. I remember waiting there in dense freezing fog for a connection to Bacup, thinking What am I doing in a miserable, dreary place like this? I almost turned back. But honouring appointments had always been important to me, so I eventually made it to India Mill in Bacup. I had lunch with managing director Arthur Duckett and Harry Holland, the main board director of Joshua Hoyle and Co.

Mr Duckett, who I came to know as A.D., was a big man with huge hands and a personality to match, and announced his pleasure at meeting a young man eager to get back into textiles.

'All I need is a job outside London,' I said. 'Anything, anywhere, doing whatever is required, whether in textiles or not.'

He laughed, and asked, 'Are you always so direct and honest and willing to risk the consequences?'

I nodded.

'That's refreshing.'

Their intention, if I agreed, was to appoint me as assistant manager to Harry Holland at a spinning mill in Bacup sometime in the new year when both parties were ready. I returned to London, relieved that I had found my way out of the city when the time was ripe.

In my quieter and more reflective moments, I have often wondered whether I might have remained in London a while longer, perhaps even indefinitely, had there been no 'threat' of being tied down in marriage. The kind and wonderful people at Pantries were gradually drawing me in against all my inclinations to live in London. I could never have had a better introduction to a first job in the city and that memory will always sustain me.

When the firm offer finally came from Joshua Hoyle, it was not for a job at Bacup, but a post as assistant weaving manager at Derker Mill, one of their other mills in Oldham. A.D. had been persuaded by the Ashworth brothers that my former experiences had equipped me for almost any management post in textiles — or elsewhere — and I was never going to argue with that.

Giving my notice to leave Pantries was not easy, made harder by the reaction of Mr and Mrs Sibley, who immediately asked me into their office and tried to persuade me to change my mind. I explained that it was tougher than I had realised to acclimatise to life in the big city, and asked them to forgive me for leaving after such a short time. I really meant it, and thanked them for all their kindness. They could not have been more understanding. They said they were sorry to lose me and wished me well for the future.

When I returned to my desk, Keith seemed amazed that his uncle and aunt had actually sent for me and even more surprised when I recounted what had happened. He said that never in the history of the company had they ever done that.

He said, 'Please think carefully and change your mind because they obviously have a high regard for you and your future with this company is assured.'

When she heard about the offer to move north, Norah was distraught. She begged me to stay in London and marry her. She made me promise to send my new address, and said she would write and continue trying to change my mind, convinced that I would never like it anywhere else.

The move north was to change my life dramatically, but who can see into the future.

24

JAMES GREAVES ('OWD DERBY)

My appointment as assistant weaving manager at Derker Mill early in 1950 appeared to be just another job on my intended peregrinations, but would prove to be the most important move of my life. Both Derker Mill and my new home were to influence the rest of my private and working life, and founded the basis for relationships that endure to this day.

Tom Bracewell, my new boss, was small, slim, energetic and bright, and made me feel welcome from our first meeting. He suggested that a room at the Manor House could serve as my new abode, a place where only male residents were accepted subject to approval by the landlady, Miss Jones. Inexplicably, the lady waived her usual formality of having tea with her prospective house guest, and accepted me immediately.

I duly arrived with my luggage and knocked on the solid, old front door. It was opened by a tall bearded man.

I said, 'Can you help me with my trunk?'

He replied, 'Why, are you an elephant?'

From that moment Roy Stanton became a friend for life up to his death in 2009 aged 85.

In its heyday, the Manor House, built in 1642 — with several additions over the years — would have been a beautiful dwelling with stables, tennis courts, large gardens and bells in the pantry to summon family retainers. All these features remained, but were disintegrating before our eyes. The courts were overgrown, the roof leaked, the stables housed an array of old cars and motorcycles, and the gardens cried out for more attention, yet somehow it still retained its character and charm. However, the gang of young men living at my new home proved helpful and resourceful. They introduced me to members of the local business world, to sporting events, lent me their bicycles, and took me all over the country by motorcycle and car.

Despite the warm welcome I received in Oldham, I had not yet fully put my past behind me. Every day for months a letter arrived from Norah Morris asking me to return to Pantries, and no doubt her waiting arms too. I do not exaggerate; I received a letter every single day without fail. "I want you to come back... Pantries would welcome you back... Come back and marry me... You can't possibly be happy in the north... Please, please, come back..." and various repetitions along those lines. My replies gradually became less frequent and eventually dried up altogether, but hers went on for at least six months. Those daily letters waiting for me on the hall mat left me feeling sad, guilty and worried about her state of mind, but I honestly had never offered encouragement in the direction of romance, marriage or life entanglements.

Back at work, Tom taught me all I needed to learn about the processes and terminology in weaving, the fabrics we wove, our markets, how weavers were paid by results, and how to cost our products.

Derker Mill in 1950 was an old and unusual building, with a history, embellished by time, about 'Owd Derby', who originally owned the place. Before my time it had been absorbed into the textile group of Joshua Hoyle and Sons. It was his old derby hat that earned him the soubriquet and I learned that tales of his meanness were exaggerated because he hid his kindness and sense of humour behind a gruff exterior. The structure of the building was rambling and spacious with the spinning processes confined to the main building and the enormous weaving shed built behind. Most mills either spun yarn or wove cloth. Derker was in a minority; it did both.

The office I shared with Tom sat two floors up overlooking Derker Street. We were directly above the general office where six staff perched on stools worked at a high sloping desk that ran the whole length of the office.

The language, and accent, barriers soon became apparent. My first question concerned an invoice with two lines drawn diagonally across and "ERA" written in between.

'It's an error,' explained Doreen, an office girl.

Her companion looked at it, tut tutted, and said, 'It should be spelled E-R-R-O-W.'

Tom Bracewell accompanied me around the noisy weaving shed where it was impossible for normal speech, so I leaned close to his ear to comment on an attractive redhead a few rows away. Shortly after our return to the office a message was relayed to me that she would be delighted if I wanted to take her out any time. It was my first lesson in lip reading; the weavers were all experts!

Tom took me home to meet his wife Clara, and children Colin and Anne who were at Hulme Grammar School in Oldham. I later met his son Alan who was reading medicine at Cambridge. Their mother taught English, and used progressive teaching methods for reading. She was very kind and gentle and treated me like one of the family.

After an interview with Ernest Lord, the main board director in charge of our group of mills, Tom asked, 'How has your salary been resolved?'

I replied that Mr Lord seemed such a nice person that I left it to him.

'I should have warned you about him,' Tom said. 'He is the meanest man, and will give you the lowest salary possible.'

He was right, but at that time my income was not relevant.

The cloth warehouseman, Harold Potts, was a giant. He wore thick spectacles, walked and spoke quietly and slowly, but his presence could be felt wherever he was in the room. A remarkable man, he had fought in the First World War where his strength and physique was once used to haul a heavy gun across rough terrain when horses were unavailable. Intelligent and well read, he had a smattering of a few languages and was a good listener. By the time I met him he was near retirement, but he was still a powerful man both physically and mentally, and someone I was privileged to know and call a friend.

Any workplace that has 400-500 employees inevitably throws up a handful of interesting characters and Derker was no exception. Ned Kershaw, Jimmy Tetlow, Fred Brierley and Harold Hill please take a bow.

Harold was a stocky, unassuming stoic with a heavy flat-footed gait who was to figure twice in life-changing decisions for me without ever realising the enormity of his impact.

Fred Brierley looked considerably older than his actual age of about 60, perched at a small, high desk in the cloth warehouse near the loading bay. Imagine a small, almost toothless elderly man with wispy hair, wearing a tattered coat that would disgrace a scarecrow, constantly peering short-sightedly at his lists. You may feel sorry for him, which I did initially. But after I took an interest in him, I learned that he was a very wealthy man who by modern standards would qualify as a millionaire, but he was incapable of spending money because he had never known how. He limited his pipe tobacco to one ounce of St Bruno a week, refusing to buy more because of the cost. He never visited a dentist or renewed his spectacles for the same reason, and always complained about his tax deductions on his pay packet.

He would proudly display his old boots. 'Sithee,' he would say, 'I've had yon boots for fifty year and they're still sound.' Or, 'Me brother put fifty quid in bank when I were twenty-one and I never touched a penny of it ever, just kept adding to it and investing the money.'

He owned and let a row of cottages on both sides of a local street, invested in embryo companies (with advice) that had grown into large ones, and re-invested all his returns with others. He lived alone in a small cottage on which he spent nothing.

'Fred, why don't you give up work and travel round the world,' I ventured.

'Nay, I canna do that, it would do no good, it would hurt me to spend.'

'Right Fred, then you can give me three thousand pounds and never miss it.'

'Nay, that's against my religion,' he said.

'Okay, then just lend me the money instead,' I said, leading him on.

After a very long pause, he said, 'I would lend thee the money because I can trust thee, but I would not trust anyone else.'.

I was flattered.

'Fred, I don't want your money. Why don't you wrap it in a sack and bury it for all the good it is to you.'

He agreed with me, sad that he was forced to accept the truth, but admitted he could never change.

It did not take too long for me to discover that what really needed to change was the attitude of everyone at the top of the company, especially those at the huge, overstaffed head office in Manchester, where no one appeared to understand the dynamics of what was needed for a successful business.

25

A PILE OF SCRAP

The chapter title refers to the Francis Barnet Cruiser, a 250cc hand-change motorcycle that I bought from David Muir for £11. 'A pile of scrap' may also have described some of the machinery in Derker Mill too, but let's start with the bike.

David, an engineering student at Manchester University, was a fellow tenant at the Manor House. He refused financial help from his parents because they had upset his older brother when he accepted a job away from his home in Scotland after completing his degree, by accusing him of ingratitude. He did not want to be 'in hock' to them, so he struggled along, denying himself all normal student pleasures and concentrating solely on getting a good degree. To escape temptation to go out on the town, David would change into his pyjamas immediately on coming in and keep them on till dawn.

One day he said that he needed to 'upgrade' his bike because it was his sole and cheapest means of transport. He persuaded me to buy it.

The Francis Barnet motorcycle really was tied together with string; nothing ever worked properly. It was very heavy for a small-engined bike and could only accelerate to 47 mph flat out. It required great caution to ride because it was almost impossible to stop safely at that speed. The foot brake touched the ground when it was only half applied, and the gearbox moved back and forth while selecting a gear, which made every change fun and took a certain amount of guesswork as to which gear would be available. They were never all available at one time. The gear lever frequently came off in my hand. Front forks needed checking constantly because they worked loose and threatened to part company with the bike; the tank leaked its petrol and oil mixture; and the headlights were so pathetic that I had to pass a hand in front to check if they were working. Whenever I kicked it into life it would explode in clouds of black smoke. All in all, Francis was a real mess, but incredibly it kept going. Except, that is, when I took it to Wales, the one place that David warned me never to ride it.

'Don't ever go there,' he said, 'it hates Wales and will refuse to respond.'

'How can an inanimate object like Francis know where it is? That's crazy.'

But every time I went to Wales, without exception, it broke down. Once I threatened to push it over a cliff when I became so exasperated. It travelled 1,000 miles a month for a year (after a fashion), but was only ever awkward on the four or five occasions I went to Wales.

And all that time I did not even have a full licence. I never dared apply for one on that heap.

Back at work, all the Lancashire looms were being converted, at enormous cost, to semi-automatics so that a weaver could run 12 looms instead of the usual four. When I suggested to our visiting technical director that semi-automatics were a waste of money, he sneered, 'What does an inexperienced young man know about these things?'

Tom Bracewell had warned me that no one at the mill ever listened to advice, and he was right. I had earlier advised against our three old sizing vats being swapped for two smaller modern versions, insisting that we would still need three large ones again. It gave me no satisfaction that eventually I was proved right after all that time and money was wasted.

With these difficulties a daily effort, why did I stay on at the mill? As always I had grown close to several people, I was learning something new, I could always move on when and if things changed, and the Manor House was a great place to live. All my deeper instincts anchored me there, even if I was unaware of what awaited me in the future.

Tom Bracewell's wife, Clara, became terminally ill about this time, and he spent as much time as possible with her. After her death he went downhill very quickly; he was unable to survive without her. When I visited him in hospital six months later he looked so bright-eyed and fresh that I believed he had turned a corner, but he passed away quietly that night. I was really distressed, losing a new-found family much too soon.

Following Tom's death, none of our group or technical directors contacted me, so I just took on the responsibility of running the weaving mill without any additional remuneration (it never crossed my mind), and took important decisions unaided by anyone more senior.

A buyer called and asked if we could sell him some fents: cut-off pieces of faulty fabric of various lengths, between 10 inches and 10 yards. Our cut-offs had previously been thrown into a side room and ignored, so I took him in there for a root around.

Back at my office he made his offer. 'One thousand to the company and one thousand in cash for you.'

Guessing that it was worth a bit more than that, I said, 'Make out a cheque for two thousand-five hundred to the company and collect the fents when it's cleared.'

With an expressionless face he complied without argument, said thank you tonelessly, and departed. In the early 1950s £1,000 cash could have bought a modest house, but I never even mentioned the incident to anyone else. That buyer climbed the business ladder, and eventually became a successful force in the textile world, the CEO of a major group, and a very wealthy man.

Perhaps the most important commercial event that ever took place during my time at the mill concerned a complaint about our main product — sheetings, many thousands of yards long. A roll of grey sheeting arrived one day with a note that all our cloth was faulty and it would cost the company a substantial sum in compensation. I was baffled because I knew that we had a strict regime of 'cloth looking' (our version of quality control) before despatch. With Harold Potts in charge I was sure that no faulty fabric would ever leave the mill. I asked him to examine the roll; he too was puzzled. The cloth width, reed and pick construction of 60X60 and 20X20 yarn count all matched our specifications, yet the fabric was full of faults. I had no doubt in my mind that it was not sheeting woven in our mill, but it seemed impossible to prove otherwise. That night I lay awake trying to think of a solution.

The following day, after examining the cloth, I had an idea. What about the selvedge, the finished edge of the cloth? It was so insignificant and narrow that it was worth examining. I cut out one edge and very carefully separated the finer yarns that formed the selvedge, laying them individually side by side on a piece of paper, about 24 in all, and held them down with Sellotape. Then I went into the drawing-in room to see Harold Hill.

'Harold, how long have you worked here?'

'All my working life, at this job,' he said

'Has our selvedge ever been altered?'

'Never,' he said, 'it's been the same for years.'

'Please show me the yarns used.'

When he did, my heart leapt. It was completely different to the pattern on the paper, which had no coloured threads of fine yarn in it as ours did. I showed it to him and he shook his head.

'Nothing like ours,' he said.

Checking back with the high-speed beamers, I was shown their creels (frames on which the bobbins are fitted) loaded with those special finer yarns at the edges — exactly those ends that Harold had to pack into each end of the reeds for the weavers' beams. That was sufficient evidence.

When I phoned head office and told them the cloth was not ours, they did not believe me, and asked how I could be so sure.

'I am prepared to stand up in court and produce evidence that it's not our cloth,' I said.

When I finally convinced them that I could back my statement, the bosses were overjoyed, and admitted relief that I had not just saved Joshua Hoyle an immense claim, but also the possibility of losing ongoing government contracts on which they depended. I silently thanked the late Tom Bracewell for devising a special signature selvedge and sticking to it, and noted that my examination of the cloth was with the pick counter he had given me, one I still have today. I have often wondered if anyone else would have thought to compare the selvedge.

Despite the fact that my intervention sent my stock sky-high, no official acknowledgement was ever made, no one visited to thank me, and no offer of an increase in salary was mentioned. But at the time, as usual, thoughts of extra remuneration never crossed my mind.

26

GOOD MORNING, MR POTTS

Only in hindsight and at my advanced age has realisation dawned that I always considered people far more important than financial rewards in any job I ever had, and that leaving those I worked with always left me with a greater loss than any lost income. Putting it simply, my real love in life was and still is a need for the company of homo sapiens of all ages of either sex, regardless of ethnicity, educational background or of their standing in society. Nevertheless, I did not want to become permanently attached to one person, which might risk being able to associate freely with everyone else. The one who changed my attitude (more than a bit) came much later in life, and who, with a literary nod to Lorna Doone, called me 'slow John Ridd'. That person is yet to appear in this narrative but she proved to be the wisest and most perceptive person I ever met.

But first, Manor House and 'Owd Derby' were so pivotal in my life that I need to dwell a while longer with them.

R.J. Stanton, Michael Clark, Chez Atkins, David Muir, Harry Hellmann, Darrell Shaw, 'Batch', Jack Saxon, Eric

Taylor, Murray French, WCS Morgan, Ron Worcester and several others made up the 'gang' at the house. Each one was very different in character and temperament, which made for an interesting mix at the house. They were, in different ways, to play a larger or smaller part in how the rest of my life would proceed.

Michael was a dreamer but also a mathematical genius who gave David Muir all his spare time to help with his degree studies. Michael was generous with his time with me too by taking me all over Britain on his motorbike. Chez dragged me along (willingly) to play centre at lacrosse for Oldham and Werneth Lacrosse Club. Others became good friends, and two of them radically changed the career path of my life. Most had influential family connections, some with first and further degrees from universities that included Oxbridge, two held former army ranks of major and captain, and at least three would be inheritors of successful family businesses.

Whenever a newcomer arrived, I would make him welcome, find out about his interests then introduce him to like-minded tenants and leave them to it, always acting as a bridge between people. My willing role as an enabler was developing without any awareness that it would prove crucial in every area of my future life.

At work I was slowly able to make some significant changes to the way some things were run. When Ernie Rostron was off sick, no one could understand how to calculate weavers' earnings because his system was so complicated. I took the lot home and devised a really simple way of doing them. I promised to work with him until he got the hang of it, which pleased him and he was grateful that his job was made so much easier. I told him that as he was near retirement age, the time saved could be used to help others, and that he was not to worry about job security. Those were the days when I started learning about getting around company regulations that stifled good relations, and realised that trust engendered much better cooperation in the workplace. In return Ernie gave me one piece of advice: 'Never treat your feet harshly by scrubbing them [which I did], but wash and rinse them well and keep them dry.' Advice I took.

My only contact with managing director Arthur Duckett was a request that I visit one of our mills in the Bacup area every Wednesday for about three months and write a report on certain events happening there, which I did. By the end of that time the mill manager was sacked, which didn't surprise me. I was sure that similar poor working practices existed at many of the other sites, confirming my opinion that no one at Joshua Hoyle really had a finger on the pulse. One of the reasons was that A.D. had too many other interests, one of them being Blackburn Rovers Football Club.

I had already paid back more than the fare paid by James Purdie for my sea trip to Tilbury before 'splashing out' on that abominable scrapheap of a bike, but found that I never wanted much money to live because my needs were simple. However, Chez Atkins persuaded me to buy a few bits of clothing from local stockists that made me look less like a country yokel.

'William,' he said, 'you don't have to spend much to look civilised. I know you don't care about success, but give it a chance.'

Then he enrolled me in the Junior Chamber of Commerce so he could introduce me to some influential people in the town. Alas for his attempts to propel me towards fame and fortune. I found some of his business colleagues pompous and self-seeking.

'I can't stand some of them,' I told him.

'Never mind, just bite your tongue, and use them as stepping stones.'

'But that's not what I want from life,' I replied.

'You will never succeed,' he said, 'because you don't care about success. But I will, even if I have to step on your toes to do it.'

And he meant it.

Despite his attitude, we got along as friends, often stopping off at the 'chippie' at the top of Park Road after our Tuesday evening lacrosse club meetings. We described the meetings as attending a 'service' with the Rev. Norman Ferguson, landlord of the George Hotel on Hollins Road. Those committee meetings were warm and friendly, and we actually achieved a lot.

Walking down Abbey Hills Road to the Manor House eating chips out of newspaper he would chuckle.

'If they could see me now, I wonder what they would think,' he said, referring to his elegantly attired office colleagues.

'They would be envious,' I said.

An instrument used in the weaving process, known as a buffalo hide picker, always fascinated me. It took a lot of pounding in the loom. Firstly it stopped the metal-nosed shuttle, then shunted it back across the loom at speed to the one waiting on the other side. They were very durable and lasted for years. One day a salesman arrived and said that he could produce buffalo hide pickers in hard plastic. I was curious and invited him to bring one in. It looked and felt good, but lasted about two minutes on the loom before breaking in half. He was stunned and asked if he could try again, with each new one lasting only slightly longer than the last. He eventually gave up.

Old Ned Kershaw was the older brother of Herbert, company secretary, and the expert on tape sizing, where warp yarn had to be given a coating of size to stand the rigours of passing through reeds and healds in the loom. Visiting textile scientists admitted that his sense of touch, smell and sheer experience were more dependable than all their expensive instruments. He knew precisely how much more sago, tragasol or china clay needed adding or removing by smelling and tasting the mix. However, his expertise went far beyond the basics. Once he was off work for personal reasons and his workmates could see that something was wrong with the mix, so they contacted him for advice.

'When it rains,' he said, 'the mixture is too weak, so make it stronger.'

'Why?' said Fred, baffled.

'Because the roof leaks and rainwater weakens the mix by dripping into the tanks,' he said. No one else knew that after all those years.

One of our lighter moments followed a visit by the factory inspector, who spotted that a heavy wooden beam had a small section cut out to accommodate a driving belt. He insisted that it was dangerous and required reinforcement, regardless of the fact that it had been like that for over 30 years. Incredibly, about 10 days after his visit, the beam collapsed. I heard one of the workers say, 'If yon man had said nowt, it would have been reet.'

Going barefoot during my growing years may have been responsible for my broad feet with high arches, so finding shoes that fitted properly was difficult in the 40s and 50s. Painful ingrowing toenails were my reward — running about for long spells at lacrosse made them worse. Someone at Derker suggested I see the young visiting chiropodist who had a session every Wednesday in our welfare department. I had previously seen her occasionally crossing the floor of the cloth warehouse being greeted by Harold Potts.

'Good morning, Miss Rogerson,' he would say.

'Good Morning, Mr Potts.'

Always the same courtesies, with a warmth that indicated genuine regard for each other. Apart from that I knew nothing about her and had never spoken to her. I made an appointment through our welfare officer on her first free slot.

27

SLOWLY TIPTOE

Messing about with my own toe did not endear me to my new chiropodist. Yes, I had made a mess of attempting to crudely dig out the offending growth with a pair of scissors, leaving a painfully swollen and ugly digit. But no comment was offered until she had finished treating it.

'If you do anything more to it before your next visit, I will be unable to treat it,' she said.

Hoity toity, I thought.

'It will need several visits to clear it up,' was her parting shot.

I thought, *I hope it's over quickly.*

But it was not. It took many, many more appointments with Miss Rogerson — I always just addressed her as 'Miss' — before she pronounced that no more could be done at that time.

She must have been able to conceal her real self very skilfully behind a cool facade for a long time, perhaps all her life, because she was maybe the only person I ever met who had me fooled so completely. It could be that I did not really look too hard or that she did not interest me beyond her capacity as a chiropodist, but even in hindsight I honestly can't remember much else except that I was attempting to deal with other problems at work.

My wish to avoid serious involvement, especially with the opposite sex, had not diminished, but in my innocence I honestly believed that being friendly with anyone at all should be accepted as precisely that, just friendship. I dismissed all thoughts of marriage as utterly absurd, and believed that no female with an ounce of common sense could ever visualise wedlock with such an impractical, destitute and unworldly person like me — least of all a cold, unyielding person like Miss Rogerson. In short, I was utterly safe with her, and she with me.

Ingrowing toe nails have a habit of continuing to do precisely that, and need more attention, so I was forced to return to Miss Rogerson's 'safe house' several weeks later. The revelation of suddenly discovering a hidden gem behind that barrier was a shock, one so unexpected and astonishing that I wondered how my renowned sixth sense had not picked up on it sooner. I cannot ever remember changing my mind so radically about anyone before, and perhaps I may have reacted like a pendulum and gone to the other extreme out of sheer exuberance and joy — and also to make amends (either to my conscience or, subconsciously, to hers, I'm not sure).

However, I must emphasise that I honestly thought we could be good friends, nothing more than that. Anything deeper was out of the question. Writing about how our relationship 'crept up' on me has not been easy simply because I have always been blind to see what everyone else can see — a particular kind of blindness connected to a personal naivety.

About that time I happened to book a holiday to Cork, in Ireland, to visit Mrs Jessop, the widow of Bill Jessop with whom I had been friendly in Bombay. Miss Rogerson, or Joan as I then knew her, asked if I could bring her back a pair of nylons, which were difficult to get in the UK at that time because we still suffered shortages following the war. (Incidentally, my ration book had been lodged with Miss Jones at the Manor House, and the meagre ration of sugar for each person was on the table with our initials on the lid. Mine read "BBC", courtesy of David Muir, who explained that it stood for Burma Bill Cribb.)

The entire holiday to Ireland, including travel, cost just £5. Michael Clark offered to drop me off at the Fishguard ferry terminal by motorbike on his way to Mumbles, where his parents were living, and pick me up on his way back to Oldham on my return. He was that kind of person, always helping friends. I had no cabin on the ferry crossing, but was invited by a group of cyclists to sleep under the tarpaulin that covered their bicycles on deck, where I slept soundly.

Southern Ireland was a really friendly place, which was shown before I had even reached my destination: Bishopstown, a neighbourhood in Cork city. I asked the bus guard to put me off somewhere near the address I had been given. He asked the passengers where exactly the address was located. Their response took the bus off the designated route and deposited me outside the door of the Jessop residence. The bus driver even waited until I had knocked and been admitted to the house. They all waved to me as the bus set off again!

The only person home was Mrs Jessop's daughter, Pat, and she had some bad news.

She said, 'I'm sorry, but Mum is in hospital in Buttevant. She's very ill and unlikely to survive.'

So off I went to the hospital by train and saw Bill's widow. I only saw her once, but at least I did see her before she died, and she was so pleased that I had been.

During my stay, Pat hired me a bicycle and we cycled around quite a large area, taking in Blarney Castle to see the Blarney Stone. The keeper invited me to kiss it, which involved lying on my back and leaning back to reach the fabled stone over a steep drop, but I refused. He wouldn't let up.

'Maureen O'Hara came to kiss it,' he said, and then added, 'I'll hold your legs so you won't fall.' But this was before health and safety regulations insisted on safety bars below.

'I don't care if the Queen herself came to kiss it,' I said, 'I'm not kissing it.'

'You don't need to kiss it,' he replied, 'you've got enough blarney already.'

Before leaving Cork, I entered a shop selling nylon stockings. I must have looked bemused because another shopper visiting from England offered to help.

'What size do you want?' she asked.

When I shrugged, she said, 'Look around and point out a lady of a similar height and build.'

I bought a pair, then decided that I would get another pair as a gift, but would definitely charge for the pair Joan asked me to get, so as not to look too willing. I was never able to fool Joan, but naively believed I could.

28

STEPPING OUT

I continued to deal with problems at work. Those problems were made worse by being concealed behind pseudo-corporate structures, allowing inefficiencies that I could sense rather than see. These difficulties were common in large, disjointed companies. Worse than that, I became aware of systematic stealing from company assets.

The 'modernisation' at Derker entailed scrapping unwanted machine parts, a source of returned income to the company. What I did not know was that every third load of scrap was paid in cash to someone unknown and redistributed to other individuals in the shadows.

I asked the weaving shed manager, 'What's going on?'

He said, 'I thought you were in on it.' He then added. 'There's nothing you can do because our director is part of the deal.'

Why wasn't I surprised?

That manager of the weaving shed appeared one day in a new car to replace his motorcycle and sidecar, effectively robbing his employer in the process. But what really upset me was the involvement of a company director. This just confirmed my opinion that, together with all the problems besetting the textile industry as a whole, my current employer was already heading towards extinction. It was just a matter of time before the whole lot imploded.

For the record, everything I feared about the futility of those half-baked conversions sadly proved correct. A weaver who had been successfully running four looms was expected to operate 12 in a row. In that enormous shed just one man succeeded, and when I asked him, 'Can you manage this job?' he replied, 'Yes, but not for too long because it's wearing me out already.'

He was our most efficient weaver and it was obvious that no one else would ever be able to match him for speed and skill. All the other lines of looms were in disarray. Consequently, operatives were staying away from work; I could understand their problem.

The solution, according to our technical director, was to take modifications even further, compounding the problem and wasting more money because, as I have said, we would still be left with outdated machinery.

I never made sudden moves unless it was a real emergency, so I remained in my job, learning how not to do things. I visited another mill in the group and spent several hours at head office based at 50 Piccadilly in Manchester. Those visits confirmed my view that Joshua Hoyle would never survive in a changing world.

While all this was happening, Joan and I had become friendly enough for me to invite her to see an amateur production of The Pirates of Penzance. She pretended that it would mean her cancelling something else — 'I was going to wash my hair tonight' or some such — but even I could see through that.

The Gilbert and Sullivan opera was of particular interest because of a school production in which I played the police sergeant in rehearsals. Fortunately for me, our producer was suddenly called up for war service as an interpreter. I look back in amusement when I think of Monsieur Cardeaux, a Frenchman, producing an English comic opera, leaving no one else capable of taking over. To my relief, it had to be cancelled.

By this time Joan had begun visiting the Manor House to see me, naturally getting to know some other residents in the process.

On one occasion, Chez Atkins said, 'You two should get married.'

I laughed, and said that we were just friends enjoying life. Joan appeared to go along with that.

So many changes were taking place at the Manor, including new arrivals and departures. Joan met most of them, including (and what a change of policy) two women: Marion, and Jean Waller, the new Youth Organiser for Oldham. Jean had played hockey for England, and may have been a catalyst for what followed.

It can't have been more than 12 weeks after Jean's arrival when we were walking down the long drive to the house when she grabbed my hand and said, almost casually, 'We should get married. I will carry on working while you go on to university, and we can move on from there.'

Oddly, I was not surprised.

I said, just as casually, 'No, but thanks anyway. You deserve someone much better, someone with more ambition. I hope we will remain as friends.'

Joan heard about my brief encounter with Jean and suggested that she and I would make a better match.

I laughed, and said, 'I am the last person you want as a husband. There are three men who want you as a wife, all successful, all established, all with excellent prospects.'

Two of these other prospects were business associates of her father; the other was a local councillor. Joan said that none of them interested her and she refused to give up on me. Meanwhile, I remained obstinate about marriage to anyone, especially to someone I liked. Incidentally, by this time I had no idea what Joan's father did, had never met him or even been to her home.

There were more changes at the Manor House. David Muir graduated with good qualifications, was offered an engineering post in the Far East, contracted some rare tropical disease and died within the first year.

Murray French, a lodger at Manor House, was noted missing one Monday evening after most of the gang returned after home weekend visits.

I asked Eric Taylor, 'Where's Murray?'

'Dead,' he said. 'Committed suicide over the weekend. Put his head in a gas oven over a broken affair with a niece of the Duke of Hamilton.'

The news really shocked me because it was so casually delivered and so unexpectedly brutal.

Three months after the arrival at the Manor House of Fred Harrison, a mellow and happy heavy drinker, he was taken in hand by the new girl, Marion.

She said to me, 'I'll make a new man of him, and don't worry, I know you like him so I will be kind but firm and gradually reduce his intake and then marry him.'

She did exactly what she promised; I think Fred was happy to be in her care.

Following my rejection, Jean became involved with Jack Saxon, another resident at the Manor House. They too eventually married and moved to a house in Uppermill.

While all this pairing-up was going on, Joan invited me to her home at Incline Road, Hollinwood. With an assurance that her parents would be out, I agreed to come over one evening. She confessed that marrying anyone connected with her father put her off completely. Only later in life did I discover her deep-seated reasons for her attitude, but I confess that it went over my head at the time.

She repeated her proposal. 'We should get married and not waste our lives apart.'

'Impossible,' I said. 'I'm destitute and utterly lacking in ambition. I would be doing you a favour by not marrying you.'

I really meant it. I left her that evening determined to end our friendship and stay away.

29

A REAL NEW START

That period in late 1952, between refusing to consider marriage with Joan and beyond the Christmas holidays, was scary because it created a gap in my life that was filled with tension. I stopped seeing her, never spoke to her directly or even on the telephone, and generally avoided her. I was scared of the responsibility as I had always cared little about what happened to me, and neither had I any desire to become burdened with worldly possessions such as a house or car. In short, I was an utterly impractical and unworldly man. How, I thought, could I possibly become responsible for the wellbeing of someone that I liked so much?

Although we went several weeks without contact, I could sense her distress. I learned much later that she too could feel mine. 12 weeks later Joan arrived at the Manor House to see me. She looked worn out.

'This has to end,' I said, 'and you have to be sensible about life with the right person. I am not that person.'

'You are the only man I have ever wanted for a husband. I knew that from the moment we met. Trying to hide it forced me to behave awkwardly.'

'No,' I implored, 'you must be sensible and marry someone who can give you everything you deserve. Please go away, think clearly and make the right choice.'

She was adamant, refusing to be put off.

I ended by saying, 'I will give up my job and leave Oldham as a favour to you.'

She broke down and pleaded with me not to go away, but to stay and marry her. She finally got under my skin. I couldn't bear to see her so upset.

'If I agree, Joan, we will have to wait three years, save some money, and look at it sensibly.'

She disagreed.

'We will be wasting time that we should be together, and I think that we have already wasted too much of our precious lives. We need to be together now.'

'We have to be sensible, Joan. Where can we live without capital? It's not possible.'

Joan was ahead of me.

'Mum and Dad have already agreed that we can stay with them till we are able to manage.'

My heart sank. Every instinct informed me that it could not work and I told her so, but she would not be put off. Joan was so determined that I was forced to agree — but only after I stated my terms.

'We must never try to keep up with the Joneses,' I said. 'We will remain very poor for a long time. We must start saving from today, open a bank account and put every penny we can spare into it, with five pounds to deposit immediately.'

I brandished the money in front of her.

And we did just that. We took the £5 to Lloyds Bank and saw Mr Lewthwaite, the manager, who would later become a friend.

I would not be the only breadwinner, of course. Joan's employer was John R Hall, first president of the Association of Chiropodists, an organisation he was instrumental in founding. His surgery, perhaps the largest one at the time, employed six full-time chiropodists. He also owned several shoe shops in the area, thus being responsible for many feet that trod the streets of Oldham. I learned later that John was a director and shareholder in the company run by her father, Ernest Rogerson, who was the sole executive director. The third shareholder was William Robertson.

John had earlier expressed a wish to marry Joan, but even without the dominating presence of his sister Mary (who terrified all suitors) she would have rejected his proposal. He was a kind and gentle man who was unable to cope with Mary.

I had also told Joan that we needed to set a date, and allow several months for the arrangements. Our wedding was finally arranged for 12th September 1953 at St Margaret's Church, Hollinwood, close to her home. Father Willis (it was Anglican High Church) treated us with great courtesy and kindness during our meeting to arrange everything and made me feel relieved about at least one aspect of that big event in my life.

Up to this point, Joan had been handing over her entire income, a reasonable one for a Glasgow University-trained chiropodist, to her parents, who allowed her 10 shillings a week for her expenses. After announcing our intention to marry, that allowance was doubled to £1, which allowed us to save a bit extra. By the time 12th September arrived, we had managed to accrue our first £100.

I left all the wedding arrangements to Joan and her parents, and never questioned any details. About this time I got to know and love Joan's auntie and uncle, Alice and Theo Rogerson, who lived in Royton. Theo, her father's older brother, never said much about his younger sibling; they were chalk and cheese. Despite their reticence, I got the impression that the brothers did not see eye to eye about most things, which worried me about my future father-in-law.

With no knowledge of the wedding details, all I could do was ask Michael Clark to be my best man. Joan asked Eva Wolstenholme to be her bridesmaid.

In order to buy my wedding suit I was forced to sell my motorbike — and actually made a profit of £1 on that heap of scrap because the buyer was proposing to rebuild it. Michael and I then went to the same tailor in Oldham to have our suits made, which were perfectly adequate.

We were not to know then that the wedding arrangements would be overturned by unforeseen events. I can only record the little I know.

Ernest Rogerson's habit of using cash meant that he had accumulated a large sum to pay for the wedding, money he kept in a drawer at home. He chose that time to redecorate, probably in preparation to receive wedding guests. But somehow the decorators must have got wind that there was cash in the house, possibly when Ernest paid them. The following day he discovered all the money missing, along with jewellery and watches from the same drawer. The thieves apparently gained entry through a window in the extension, perhaps left unlatched during the working day for them to return later.

That loss proved to be a black mark against me even before Joan and I were married because, without actually saying anything to me, I knew that he disapproved of his daughter marrying a penniless man.

I discovered later that he was convinced I had planned to marry her to inherit his money.

30

INNOCENTS ABROAD

When I accept and agree to something, I embrace it completely and put my heart and soul into it — there is no other way.

We declined to draw from our deposited savings for anything before our marriage, and Joan did not even have an engagement ring until I took her to Joseph Howells in Oldham and she settled happily on a simple token of engagement: marquisette stones set in a silver ring. While we were browsing, I noticed her admiring a green enamelled dragon broach. I said nothing before we left the jewellers, and then returned without her on the pretext I had forgotten something, and whispered to one of the brothers to put it aside for me.

We had already found and paid for her 22ct. gold wedding ring, and Joan was having her dress made by Elizabeth Gray in Oldham, a simple but stylish street velvet outfit in a deep wine colour.

I later picked up the broach. Then I wrote neatly on a small piece of paper:

A wish, a prayer, that stars will shine
Within your eyes, when you are mine.
But ... if you blah, by the hour
THIS will get you!

I wound the note around the dragon, placed it in the box, wrapped and sealed it and gave it to her mother with a request to hand it to Joan on the morning of the 12th.

I left all the other arrangements to Joan and her parents, burying my head in the sand to maintain my equilibrium in the certain knowledge that sooner rather than later I would be faced with real problems needing all my balance and focus. I was fortunate in not being able to see into the future.

The actual wedding group numbered eight: Joan's parents, Ernest and Ivy Rogerson, Uncle Theo and Auntie Alice, Michael Clark and Eva Wolstencroft, Joan and I.

I was polishing a pair of black shoes on my last day at the Manor House when Michael announced that the taxi had arrived. Only when we reached the church did I notice black shoe polish on my hand. Sitting on the front pew, I used a handkerchief to wipe it off and heard later that someone across the aisle sympathised because I was so nervous — he apparently believed that my hands were wet with perspiration. Mike and I were actually discussing the architecture.

I was delighted to see Joan was wearing the green dragon broach. She beamed at me in complete understanding about my quirky verse. Even in those early days we were always on the same wavelength and explanations were never needed.

With one exception, all our wedding photos show just the eight people mentioned. But one had 16, four friends of the family from Uppermill and four others. They all came along to support us at church, but were not invited for the meal at number 8 Incline Road. It was as small and simple as any wedding could possibly be, and without comment to each other, it suited both of us perfectly.

We went off to a farm in Glynceiriog, North Wales, by bus and train for our honeymoon. On the train I asked Joan to take off her wedding ring.

Holding it in my hand, I said, 'This is just a symbol of our marriage. If you lose it please don't worry. It's just an object. We have a life together that's more important.'

Then I kissed her.

Those few days away helped me realise that we needed each other so much more in every way than I ever dreamed. That is why I named this chapter Innocents Abroad. It is difficult to believe that two grown-ups could really have been so innocent about demonstrating their love for each other as we did right from the start. Several weeks later, when Joan's pregnancy was confirmed, the estimated date for her first birth was about nine and a half months after our wedding day.

But not everything in the garden was rosy. Joan's father channelled disapproval every day through her mother to Joan, never directly to Joan and never to me. Their attitude could not have been more destructive had we been arrested for serious criminal offences. Joan became distressed on a daily basis and I often found her crying quietly. Combined with morning sickness, which was quite severe, her father's attitude was really unhelpful.

I knew with absolute certainty that we had to get away and live on our own terms, so I began a desperate search to find a place we could afford — not easy with such limited resources. We chased all over, looking at impossible dwellings that I recall now with horror, reluctant to subject my lovely wife to a life in a hovel or in some isolated wooden shack on the moors (yes, we did look at one). I kept my eyes and ears wide open hoping something would come up. We heard about a cottage to rent up the hill on Ripponden Road and dashed up there. We knocked at the address and the house next door. The door was opened by a lady who said that she owned both properties but the one to rent was already let. Joan was so upset that she burst into tears and the landlady, Mary, put her arms round her and invited us in, sat us down and made a cup of tea. We may not have secured the house but we did better than that: Mary and Arnold Wood, who had a stall in the original Oldham market hall, remained friends for many years after this surprising introduction.

For several weeks I looked for a home without success, determined that Joan needed removing from the source of her distress, i.e. her parents. The solution came unexpectedly at work on 1st March 1954. Harold Hill came into the office for instructions and mentioned his intention to live with his daughter and her husband.

Unaware of any problem, I asked, 'Why are you moving?'

'Because since I lost my wife they think I should stay with them.'

'What about your house?'

'I'm selling it, but it's not on the market yet.'

I was already getting excited.

'Where is it?' I asked.

'At Waterhead.'

My next question surprised him. 'Is there any coal in the cellar?'

'Yes, lots, we've just had a full delivery.'

'Would you be happy to sell it to me at a price agreed between us and an estate agent that we know?'

'Yes.'

'Can I move in tomorrow?'

After a short silence, Harold said, 'I trust you, so yes, you can.'

'Thank you Harold,' I said, 'we will sort things out very soon.'

I found a removal company in the directory, and phoned them.

'Please move us tomorrow morning,' I said. 'Nothing except a bed, a wardrobe, some clothes and little else, and please don't say you can't.'

They must have heard the pleading in my voice. They agreed.

I phoned Joan at work. 'We will be sleeping in another house tomorrow night. Can you stay at home, make sure everything is picked up and go with them to 171 Stamford Road. I will arrive there sometime later in the morning.'

'But we have nothing at all,' said Joan.

Then, like the incredible person she always proved to be, she said 'Right, leave it to me.'

With that, she took the rest of the day off, bought a bread bin and walked around filling it with provisions for the move. I said nothing to her parents. I know I should have done, but I could not be moved to do so.

We moved into our new home on Stamford Road the following day, 2nd March. I arrived at 11 in the morning, shortly after our few things had been delivered. The first thing I did was light a fire in the kitchen. I laid out paper, sticks and a few coals on top, then realised we had no matches. I switched on the radiant ring and used that to light a touch paper. It worked.

Harold had left an old, cast iron cooker on legs with the grill pan and some other utensils, but Joan said that she could not use the dirty grill pan. It looked impossible to restore, but I said 'Beggars can't be choosers' and set about scouring it. An hour later it looked like new. Joan was astonished. I then successfully cleaned the rest of the cooker.

Harold had also left us several other useful items: a dining table and four chairs, an ironing board, a tin bath in excellent condition, all the light fittings, a cellar full of coal, and two sound, useable fireplaces with one fireguard. He asked for £40 for the lot, and said he would wait until we could afford to pay him. It was a great start for two people who owned next to nothing.

We enjoyed exploring our new home. There were two bedrooms upstairs, a good-sized front room and a large kitchen. Down stone steps from inside the kitchen we had a large stone slab to keep things cold (and it did) and steps from the back door went past the cellar door out to the backyard, at the bottom end of which was an outside flush toilet.

I remained in the house all day, sorting, cleaning, clearing, discussing how to use our remaining capital effectively, and planning our first steps into unfamiliar domestic territory.

In the meantime, an estate agent valued the house at somewhere between £450 and £500. The following day, 3rd March, I went into work, typed out a formal receipt for £100 and gave Harold a downpayment cheque in return for his signature. We had about £40 left to buy everything else, starting with curtains, and still had to find another £40 to pay Harold for the appliances and furniture he left in the house.

We were both still earning a salary but Joan was then about five months into her pregnancy, so her time at work was limited. Provision for time off with benefits did not exist in that era, so we had to plan the arrival of our first child meticulously.

31

TOUGH TEN YEARS

Details of those 10 years at Stamford Road will follow later, but a summary of the events that took place there may enable me to put them into some kind of perspective as I continue my narrative.

During that time, the Cribb family firmly established itself in Waterhead, at that time a quiet village-style place away from the hurly burly of Oldham, with lots of open space behind the row of houses. Mike was born on 25th June 1954 in Boundary Park Hospital (now Royal Oldham Hospital), Alan was born at home on 24th August 1956, and Caroline Joan arrived on 4th March 1959, also at home. Joan stayed on at work for as long as possible before Mike's arrival, but never returned to work during those 10 years. She preferred to stay at home and be a full-time mother. I was happy about that, but warned (again) that funds would be extremely tight and our lifestyle basic, with no holidays, no TV, just the bare necessities.

On the work front, I was destined to graduate in the toughest business school possible (my first rescue operation), learn to drive, work in a building supply business, and then be recruited to rescue another failing business before being able to offer my wife and children a more comfortable lifestyle.

Without someone as special as Joan, we would never have succeeded during those tough times. Her love, patience, absolute trust and wisdom were the basis on which the family managed to win through. She was a rock. However, I must never overlook the enormous support we had from our children. They also accepted without complaint the shortage of almost everything and demonstrated a high degree of intelligence, understanding and patience rarely evident in childhood. I cannot have been easy to live with during those stressful times and they would not have been blamed for rebelling. Of course, like all siblings they had disagreements as they grew, but they seemed more concerned to share our family problems. I have always admired them for that.

However, I must repeat that Joan was the most important factor, as wife, friend, kind and considerate mother, whose wisdom and stabilising influence was pivotal in holding everything and everyone together through those very difficult years.

32

TRANSITION

From March '54 to July '57 — in spite of misgivings about certain practices at work — I remained at Derker Mill for three main reasons: it provided a steady income, my commute to work was just a short bus ride on the 98 from Waterhead terminus to Derker Street, and because we were just too busy to even think about changing jobs.

Everything previously mentioned still applied at work — no proper connection between head office and the mills, no quality at technical director level (whose only focus was on personal benefits), no realisation that eventual disaster was inevitable, and, all in all, just like Britain before the banks crashed, everyone was living happily in never-never land.

Joan and I had so much to do before Mike was born. Colin Scammell, a friend from the lacrosse club, arranged a mortgage with the Middleton Building Society on Queen Street in Oldham, after his business acquaintance from the same institution had valued the house. Colin also gave us a Silver Cross pram, which Joan and I pushed from Garden Suburbs to Stamford Road, laughing and chatting all the way, perhaps a distance of five or six miles. That pram was to serve the children well for years after I repainted it and renewed the apron. Then Arnold and Mary Wood gave us a cot that Arnold had built, delivered it to us and erected it.

It was not only children's supplies that we needed. The house also needed some TLC. I repaired several window sills and completely rebuilt one at the back with concrete, which lasted us out our time at the house.

We used the existing Water Board quarterly payment system to install an efficient, over-sink water heater for dishwashing and a freestanding boiler on legs (with a tap) for baths and laundry. Harry Nicholls, a builder, replaced the draining board with one he made to measure, and despite numerous reminders he never sent us a bill.

We made sure that Harold had been paid his £40 balance for the purchase of the house fairly quickly before 'indulging' on essentials. By 24th June we were prepared to welcome an addition to the house. At about three in the morning Joan woke and felt sure she was about to give birth. I reassured her that it was too early for that, so she went back to sleep almost instantly. She woke again at six, went downstairs and washed some clothes by hand 'to occupy my mind', she said, then we had breakfast and continued with our normal daily round. At about six thirty, I went to the phone box at the end of Stamford Road and called for an ambulance to take Joan to maternity at Boundary Park Hospital. The medical staff at the hospital dealt sympathetically with these beginners.

One said, 'It's much too early, but we will keep her in now.'
Michael was born three hours later.

172

The following morning I noticed the nurses looking at me curiously, so I said, 'What's the problem?'

'We just wanted to see this Bill your wife mentioned. Moments after the birth she sat up and said, "Can I go home to Bill now?". She will need to stay here a few days before we allow her to go home.'

I asked them to show me how to change a nappy and explain bottle-feeding because Joan was unable to produce enough milk to satisfy the baby.

Jack and Jean Saxon invited me to live with them in Uppermill while Joan was in hospital.

On the morning of the day Joan was discharged, her mother appeared at the house to help. I was not feeling well, so I went to bed and slept for three hours before Joan arrived. Her father had yet to make an appearance but we knew that he always used his wife as an ambassador and sooner or later he would show up.

Joan slept soundly that night and I woke to feed the baby when he needed it, changed his nappy, and put him back in his cot. We had a good supply of the old-fashioned cotton nappies that needed washing. We also boiled them before hanging them out to dry.

It is difficult to remember so much of what happened in those early years because there was little let-up: we had visits and help from friends like the Saxons, the Woods and others; the housekeeper from the big house on Stamford Road often brought over meals or dishes she had baked — we became good friends, not just with her but with her employer Austin

Lees and his daughter who offered an open invitation to visit at any time; our neighbours were also helpful and friendly.

Our fruit and vegetables came from greengrocers Tom and Alice Lynch on Huddersfield Road, just a short walk from home. They would often deliver the groceries with extra items, which they insisted would only be wasted over the weekend if not used, making it appear that we were helping them. As time passed they also supplied us with cash (tucked under the deliveries) as we paid more than required by cheque for the goods, thus saving us from ever going to the bank. They too became friends for life, even when they moved away from the area. I was pleased to be able to help them when our positions were reversed.

Then a business opportunity that had been bubbling under for some time was once again put to me. Harry Hellmann from the Manor House asked me several times to help him with his business ventures and contacted me again twice after I had left. He was quite insistent and said that he could only succeed with my help. His two previous attempts had failed, not because he lacked intelligence or business acumen, but because he was impatient and disorganised and rubbed people up the wrong way by refusing to accept that other people could be as intelligent or hardworking as himself. He saw me as a stabilising influence, someone who could be trusted, and knew me to be capable and hardworking. Harry had big plans, and said that I could be an integral part of his successful import and export business, and eventually become a director and shareholder with a secure financial future.

Following the death of my boss Tom Bracewell, and after running the mill alone for several months without any sign of appreciation or reward from the company, I discussed my future with Joan. She said that I had not really been challenged in my working life and was capable of achieving so much more. After our talk, I agreed to join Harry Hellman's embryo venture, which consisted of just four people: himself, his wife Mary, his secretary Winifred, and teenager Beryl Salt.

When I handed in my notice at the mill, things happened quickly. Early the following morning our technical director offered, in a manner designed to sound magnanimous, an instant doubling of salary, a further worthwhile increase when future salary reviews were held, and other expenses in connection with my job. He made me squirm, and I thought, Why wait for a letter of resignation before actually focusing on what should have been discussed months ago? I just said, 'No.'

He looked amazed at my refusal, asked me to think about it and left my office. Within the hour, Arthur Duckett telephoned and asked me to reconsider. He added that he had plans for my future with the company. He seemed genuinely upset.

Despite his reaction, I said, 'I am really grateful for all your help but feel it is time to move on after nearly seven years. Thank you again.'

He accepted my explanation and wished me well in any new ventures. I kept my true feelings about how the company operated to myself. The fact that the big chief had called me travelled round the office and suddenly I acquired a new status. It confirmed my opinion that all problems within organisations start at the top, and that the people in that place have to be seen, recognised by their employees, and really understand what is happening at all levels. That was not the case at Derker Mill, and now they had lost me.

33

P.J. HILLMAN

Mike was two years old when I began work in Manchester with Harry; Alan, my second son, was due in a matter of weeks. I have often wondered had I known then what I know now, whether I would have taken that step into a start-up company with someone like Harry. It all seemed like a straightforward challenge, but it was to prove a challenge most sane people would have avoided. However, the die was cast.

On day one Harry asked if I had a driving licence. When I said no, he insisted I get one. He asked Fritz, a young Austrian he used as a van driver, to take me on the afternoon delivery to Halle Models in Macclesfield, and allow me to drive back to Manchester. Fritz was in Manchester to improve his English in return for expenses and lodging, but his command of the language at that time was limited. After the delivery, he turned the van around, got out, and said, 'Drive'.

When I asked, 'How?' he merely shrugged. Driving back to the office in Manchester was not just a nightmare for me, but also for every unfortunate driver near the van in the rush-hour traffic. Fritz offered no help. It was a miracle we arrived without a major incident. He did say the next day that he didn't sleep that night.

The following day I applied to take my test because Harry said it would take a month to come through, by which time I would have to drive huge distances as a 'learner' driver in a variety of company vehicles: Harry's own saloon car, Mary's sports car, and the firm's two vans.

My first important job was to arrange the company's customs entries and liaise with H.M. Customs and Excise at Salford Docks and elsewhere. It took me two hours to understand the complex worksheets they required. Beryl had been struggling for weeks to understand them and was so upset with my instant grasp that she gave her notice and left her job the following week. Neither she nor Harry seemed to appreciate that it required both an ability to grapple with an unusual 'equation' and a mathematical mind. Beryl had neither, and could not be blamed for that, but this was an early occasion when I noticed that Harry was unable to 'see' either the presence or the absence of certain essential talents in most people. This was a serious flaw in his make-up because busy people should not be expected to blunder through each working day and expect success.

Additional tasks were added to my job description every day, from getting to know the Austrian and Swiss suppliers and all the embroideries they made, to customers' purchase and sale prices, from whom we bought our base fabrics to export to the 'yield' expected from them. Then I had to deal with bleachers and dyers, travel to Customs House and Salford Docks every day or to Ringway (Manchester) Airport, drop off deliveries if they happened to be on my way to or from work, and pack goods for delivery, often on my evenings off. It didn't end there. I was required to check every outgoing invoice daily against delivery notes for quantities and prices, then seal and post them at the main post office on my way home.

When I think back to those days in Manchester I must have been crazy to believe that I could endure such a furious pace. In my innocence I thought that all my effort would eventually, in time, be rewarded with better organisation of workloads, increased company income, and perhaps an enhanced personal salary to benefit my own family. Instead, my own workload and responsibilities increased in direct proportion to company growth, but my income remained static. Above and beyond those duties, my input was to offer insight, diplomacy, good client relationships and attention to detail; qualities that were lacking in Harry. Without this, P.J. Hillman would not have remained in business.

My first contact with the customs office was an education. The clearly distrustful customs officer (distrustful because of the poor relationship Harry had already established), looked at the documentation I handed him. He was tall, stern and poker-faced, and had the wonderful Channel Island name of Le Mesurier.

'Print your name in full, there!' he pointed.

'Is it important?' I asked

'When we take you to court and fine you two thousand five hundred pounds we want to make sure that we have the right person,' he said.

'You're joking,' I said.

'I never joke,' he said.

I could see he meant business, and I duly complied.

Within months we became good friends, and I asked, 'Why were you so stern and serious the first time we met?'

'Because I didn't know you and I don't trust anyone until I am sure I can.'

I took that as a compliment. I subsequently became trusted by all the customs officers because I never lied in my documentation, even when the truth created more work for me. I was rewarded with expedited entries whenever it was possible.

Every customs department operated independently, and I was lucky to have earned good working relationships with both Salford and Ringway. One landing officer at Salford said that the volume of documentation from me was greater than from anyone else, but when I told him that it was just a fraction of my workload he was astonished, and said that my salary must be massive. Explanations were pointless so I said nothing and allowed him to believe whatever he wished; but it did give me pause for thought.

Having dealt with Harry, the officers offered their sympathies about my workload. I acknowledged their concern and embellished my problems. I later told Harry what I said about him and all he said was, 'Say anything you want about me if it gets the business moving more quickly'.

That seemed to me a short-term view. He did not realise how much his reputation mattered, especially with customers and service providers. We had one fantastic freight forwarder in Europe, P. Hauser & Co., who handled all our shipments using groupage, but Harry was so impatient with them that they threatened to stop dealing with us until I promised that I would be the only person to speak to them in future. They said that if they heard his voice on the phone they would never handle anything for us ever again. They were not the only company to insist on exclusive contact with me. While it was certainly flattering, it only added to my already overcrowded workload.

Customers would ask to speak to me about the non-arrival of their goods after hearing from Harry that it had already been despatched. When I told them that their order had not even arrived in the country, Harry would chastise me for not backing him up.

'What's the point in lying,' I said, 'because they will know the truth by tomorrow anyway.'

It made no difference to his peculiar way of 'bending' the truth.

He had lots of good points, such as an ability to work very hard with inexhaustible energy, to never give up, to believe that anything was possible, to shrug off losses, and to secretly help those who had helped him in the past — something he never wanted anyone to discover because it embarrassed him. He had good business ideas, good contacts in Austria and Switzerland, and spoke five languages, at least three fluently. But his excitability and impatience almost outweighed all these plus points. Mary often disappeared from the office for several days and everyone knew why — she couldn't stand Harry.

There was one competent but difficult woman who shared an office with me and assumed that she could be rude to this busy and uncomplaining man. Since I was in and out of the place so often, I shrugged it off, but one day she went too far and I snapped. Grabbing her wrist I dragged her through the (stunned and silent) main office into Harry's place, and said, 'If you don't sort her out, I will chuck her through the window. I've had enough.'

Then I stormed off.

I think Rita had underestimated my resolve and strength when roused; the change in her attitude after the incident was astonishing. She could not do enough for me, and tried to defend me against everyone, including Harry, made me drinks, ran errands, in fact anything I wanted. Later, someone told me that she came from a rough family in Oldham where all the children were beaten by the father before leaving home, as she did. I thought, Poor lass, so unfair, no wonder she's like that.

By this time, P.J. Hillman could not function without me. That was a fact. On at least two occasions my instinct proved correct. Halle Models had been good customers from the beginning, but one day when I called with a delivery at their new premises (a large converted mill, modernised and equipped with all the bells and whistles) I had an uneasy feeling.

On my return, I said to Harry, 'What do they owe us?'

He was puzzled, 'Is there a problem?'

'I don't know, but I feel uneasy, I can't explain it.'

He looked it up, and said, 'Over twenty thousand.'

That was a considerable sum for such a small and vulnerable company as ours, so I made a suggestion.

'Shall we ask them to pay for each delivery plus £1,000; seems fair to me.'

We put it to them and they agreed, slowly paying off their balance week by week. On week 20 they went into liquidation, owing us a fraction of the original debt, about £1,250. My instinct had saved P.J. Hillman from a huge bad debt.

Harry asked, 'How did you know?'

'I didn't know, it was just a feeling.'

Another regular client was Playtex at Port Glasgow. When they requested an urgent delivery, I asked the same question, 'How much do they owe us?'

Coincidentally, it was about the same amount, just over £20,000.

This time my approach was different. I told Harry, 'No delivery until they pay all they owe us.'

He was shocked. 'We can't, they will just refuse to pay.'

'Ask them, please,' I said.

He called them and they offered to send a cheque to clear the debt.

But I said, 'No, we want a bank draft, not a cheque.'

Harry jibbed at that suggestion, but I insisted. He told them and they hung up.

'Now we have lost it all,' said Harry.

'Wait,' I said, 'they have to come back to us, our design is in their catalogue for this season and they can't get it from anyone else, at least not for a long time.'

They did come back. They sent a messenger with a banker's draft. Once that was banked, we delivered their order. As I had predicted, we lost them as customers, but we got all our money.

Had we been stiffed once for £20,000, it would have put the viability of the company in jeopardy, but twice definitely would have put us out of business. I later learned that Harry had been juggling accounts in two unconnected banks to stay afloat, using an overdraft from one to pay the other. It had been touch and go for a while. The principal bank would never guarantee us enough to pay all our customs duty by cheque, so some always had to be in cash, which created huge ongoing problems. If both Harry and Mary were away on business, he always forgot to make provision for me to withdraw cash, which meant I had to be very persuasive with the bank. I said to him that anyone else would have been unable to do what I did to keep things going.

They both went to the USA for six weeks to find new suppliers, leaving me to manage. Harry left instructions with the bank that allowed me to draw £100 every day, six days a week, so during their time away I handled £3,600, a huge sum in the fifties when annual wages were around £400-500. I could not take the chance of running out of cash so I withdrew the maximum sum every day, which meant accepting the responsibility of having large amounts on me all the time. Following his method of paying weekly wages in cash out of his pocket, I had to do the same for those six weeks.

Harry left word that Lucy should deal with customer queries, but they still insisted on speaking to me. I was the focus for everything at P.J. Hillman during their time away.

However, there was one great advantage gained by his absence. I was able to organise things my way; there was no Harry to remove relevant documents (to his home, etc., where I often had to retrieve them before entering customs documents). Despite his objections, I kept a detailed record of the customs entry numbers, dates, ships (such as the Ardetta or Bittern). What he considered to be a waste of time proved invaluable in the long run. Whenever my new 'friends' at Customs House searched for details of entry numbers and dates, even ones unconnected with us, they often phoned me for assistance. In return they were a great help in passing my documentation quickly. This had a knock-on effect on our outgoings because dock charges for goods not removed escalated rapidly, so we saved money — as I pointed out to Harry.

I kept track of all cash expenses during those six weeks on six sheets of paper. I was relieved when they returned. Mary stayed at home to recover from the journey, but Harry walked through the offices without comment for two days. Then suddenly he stopped before my desk, and said, 'Why is everything so up to date and tidy? There's nothing for me to do, it's all finished.'

'Because you were not here to muck it up,' I replied, 'it was easy.'

I told him that I could account for all the cash outgoings except for about £11.

I said, 'It was spent somewhere.'

He looked at me with a strange expression, as if to say, 'Your problem is that you are too honest for your own good.'

It was rare to see him look so sad, and to this day I never understood what he meant.

'Are you telling me that I should rob you?' I asked. He didn't reply.

Harry caused me so many problems that it is impossible to list them all, but one trip to Goole and another to Southend Airport took me towards the brink. The former I was able to solve by using tact and perseverance, but the latter, over a long weekend, nearly finished me.

A European supplier despatched via Channel Air Bridge a shipment of parcels too bulky to send by aircraft to Ringway Airport, so I travelled down to Southend in a large van on Sunday evening at a moment's notice. En route I snatched a few hours' sleep at the Saracen's Head in Chelmsford and then continued to Southend Post Office on Monday morning to collect invoices — which had not arrived. A long-winded process followed. Firstly, I phoned the office, which in turn got all the details by telex, and then I had to stand at the phone for ages, writing it all down as an invoice, which the customs office initially refused to accept. I eventually convinced them that they still had the option of checking the goods with a further option of taking an additional deposit over and above the required duty payable until the original invoices were produced. That was just the start of my problems, because they invoked the 24-hour turnaround rule for passing customs entries. I begged them to bring that forward and luckily got their agreement. Getting cash from the airport bank was my next problem because they did not know me, and had no authorisation to pay me anything at all. After pleading, showing them my previous entries for which I had to pay cash, and making a few calls, I eventually got the money.

My greatest hurdle still faced me. Customs landing officers work independently of their own office and refused to depart from their 24-hour rule.

'Come back tomorrow,' said an officer.

'But I have nowhere to go,' I pleaded, 'and Manchester is where I need to be.'

'Not our problem,' he said, 'get lost.'

I sought out and found the airport clearing agents, asking them to use their influence with officers they knew. This they did, which seemed to infuriate the customs men even more, who accused me of underhand tactics. I protested that I was tired and desperate. It didn't help.

With nowhere to go — and no goods — I sat down in front of them and refused to leave, despite repeated requests to exit the premises. I was really tired, hungry and close to despair and had stopped caring about anything they said.

After two hours of stalemate, my tormentor came into the room, and said, 'How do we get rid of you?'

'Easy, just give me what I want and I'll go, or do you really want to see me beg?'

'Yes,' he said.

I approached the desk and knelt down before him in an exaggerated begging posture.

I could see he was stunned. He turned away and summoned his colleagues from within.

'You have to come and see this,' he called.

One officer, at least, had some feeling. He said, 'For heaven's sake, George, have a heart. Just give him what he wants and let him leave.'

Normally an officer would have asked me to open three or four parcels chosen at random, but not that charmer. I had to open every single package as he painstakingly checked and counted every item, slowly and carefully, deliberately taking his time. It was very late before he finished, leaving me with the huge task of repacking and tying up the whole lot.

Before departing he simply had to rub it in. 'You can't get home tonight because the whole country north of Cambridge is covered in the densest freezing fog we've had for years,' he smirked.

The officer was absolutely right about the freezing fog. The dark, lonely unlit roads were no place for an extremely weary young man who just wished to lie down and sleep. There was not a single moving vehicle on any road I travelled, cars and vans were abandoned in every town centre I passed through. But by this time I was past caring, I just wanted to get home. I began singing with the window wide open to stay awake and to clear the windscreen to see the road ahead. Eventually I got so cold that I had to stop and sleep in the car. But even with the heater on I got too cold and moved off again. This happened several times and my journey proceeded in stops and starts all through the night, somehow managing to arrive at Harry's house at seven in the morning. I locked the van and drove his car home where Joan looked at me in horror. I was in such a state that she had to help me upstairs where I stretched out on the bed and instantly fell asleep until three that afternoon. When I got up, Joan said that she hardly recognised my drawn and weary face, which was still black with soot from the fog. That trip to Southend was the greatest waking nightmare of my life, and I vowed that I would never do it again for anyone.

Turnover at P.J. Hillman was growing. We were taking on more staff and needed more storage space, so we took another warehouse on the other side of the lift. Of course, my workload increased in direct proportion. My life was becoming work-bound, while my time at home steadily diminished. I was growing weary of the routine of work, travel and sleep. Subconsciously it began seeping through to me that it had to end soon, but I was so brain-tired that it was impossible to focus on a solution — even when two of our customers offered me a job. One said that I would be appreciated by them much more than by Harry, and that we could share all the rewards of working together. I liked the customer and I confess to being tempted by his offer, but somehow I still had a soft spot for that impossible man, so I carried on as usual. That is, until something happened to force my hand.

34

LIFE AT HOME

During this frantic time my lovely wife had been coping without complaint, even though I returned home every evening too tired or too busy to help very much, often with customs entries to finish so they could be handed in the next morning. My business life had become very intrusive, but I always tried to ensure that I had half a crown left at the end of the week to buy fresh fruit from a stall to take home. Looking back, it was incredible how much you could get for half a crown in the late fifties and early sixties.

As expected, Joan's father duly turned up at Stamford Road, but it was not long before he began criticising the house and the way we were living our lives, telling us what and how we should be doing things.

I said, 'You will always be welcome here but please don't tell us what to do. If you insist on trying to run our lives I would rather you stayed away.'

He turned to Joan for support. 'Are you going to allow him to speak to me like that?'

I knew that she still felt like a dutiful daughter, so I was pleased when she said, 'Sorry, Dad, but Bill is my husband, and this is now my home and my family.'

Speaking directly to him, I said, 'Joan is free to disagree with me or anyone else and I can't allow anyone to take that away from her. We must respect her as wife, mother and person in her own right. She deserves no less.'

He had never been crossed before by either his wife, Ivy, or by his daughter, and he did not like this new challenge to his authority. He soon left, taking Ivy with him.

I consoled Joan. 'It may be another week or two but they will return,' I said. 'I am the stumbling block in this marriage and he will never accept me as his son-in-law, but we have our own lives to lead, however difficult.'

When he eventually returned, I really tried very hard to meet him more than halfway, not because I wanted anything from him, but simply to keep relationships on an even keel. At times he gave the impression of agreeing with my point of view, but it never lasted very long. His habit of dominating the people around him had become too ingrained along with his unshakeable belief that my co-operation was governed by a wish to inherit his wealth. Mother-in-law Ivy was never a problem; she was really sweet and kind but had to behave as demanded by Ernest in order to survive — in much the same way that Joan had always conformed to support her mother.

Life started to get even tougher about the time Caroline was born in 1959; even Harry could see I was stressed. He knew we had been invited to stay with Uncle Theo and Auntie Alice in Fareham, Hampshire, where they had moved to live in a new bungalow, so he offered to pay return train fares for the family from Central Station. I accepted his offer. Our baby daughter travelled in her portable carrycot and at least we had a week of relaxation together. Harry promised to leave a vehicle outside the office for our return journey, a short walk from the station.

Sure enough, there was a van parked where he promised it would be. But of course this was Harry, and he had a surprise waiting for me. He had left a note in the van asking me to make a delivery to a customer in Stalybridge on my way in to work the following morning. I looked behind me and the van was stuffed so full with rolls of fabric that there was no space for the family. I was so angry that I very nearly walked away from it there and then because everybody — plus luggage — had to squeeze into the front. I managed to calm down and decided to confront him next morning about his thoughtlessness. With him, nothing else but business ever mattered.

I soon discovered that while I was away he had been storing up a lot of unfinished business. Customs work awaited my return and matters with bleachers and dyers needed urgent attention. Finding relevant documentation was a major time-waster with, as usual, some of it at his house. It took at least two weeks of hard work for me to clear the backlog.

The company had expanded so much — our annual turnover was approaching £500,000 by this time — that we were outgrowing even our expanded premises. A major move was forced on us, and we eventually found a full floor of space in an empty former mill on Pollard Street, Manchester. It should go without saying that I was the main organiser for planning the construction of office space, warehousing areas, reception and despatch. Fortunately I had help from a young surveyor friend, Mike Hannen, who knew the pressures I was under. He drew up plans and blueprints after we had discussed areas to inspect fabrics (for best light) and he did it all free as a personal favour to me. I have never forgotten him or how he supported me.

Then we had to construct the shelving, most of which was done (apart from the main divisions) by ourselves, and took weeks of working after-hours. The heaviest job of all came with the move itself, loading and unloading two large warehouses of stock and — guess what — once again after normal hours by two or three of us. Step one, fill the lift, step two take it down to the loading bay, step three load the vans, step four drive across Manchester. Then reverse the first three steps and carry it all up to the third floor. It is impossible now to recall how many times we did that or how long it took, but it was a mammoth task, especially after completing a full day's work. I became a walking zombie. I had fooled myself into believing it was my own business, and never received an extra penny for all the extra time, despite being promised so much at every stage. Just when we had almost completed the move, it happened.

After an exhausting evening I went home straight to bed and for the first time overslept and got to work around ten o'clock. Harry began ranting at me about how he had been waiting for the van.

'How can we work without the van when you come in so late!'

He went on and on like a demented man, but I was already walking away. I carefully picked up my things and walked out of the office and took the bus home. As I walked up from Waterhead back to Stamford Road, I saw Joan coming towards me holding our small daughter. Her face lit up.

'You've left him,' she said. 'Thank God. This is a great day.'

'Look at me,' I said, 'your husband has no job, no money and has a wife and three children to support. It's crazy.'

'You're alive, and that's the most important thing,' she said. 'Any longer, and I would have lost you. We can survive anything now and I can get work.'

Without further discussion, she went straight out and got a job at Park Cake Bakeries on the production line for chocolate éclairs. She worked her first shift that evening. What a wonderful wife.

35

SAMUEL GRATRIX

There was no time to waste. I immediately wrote seven letters enquiring about vacancies. Then I scoured the local papers. When that was done I visited the local Labour Exchange. There were crowds milling around at ground level so I went upstairs and was ushered into a small cubicle where I faced a young member of staff.

She looked sad. 'Did you notice the numbers downstairs?' she asked. 'It's a bad time for vacancies and there are no jobs at all.'

'But,' I insisted, 'someone somewhere must have a job.'

'Yes, but not for someone like you.'

'Ha, so there is something available. What and where is it?'

Again she repeated, 'Not for you.'

'Please tell me, I have a family to support and I am capable and willing to do anything at all.'

There were two jobs going: a porter was required at Mumps Station, and a company was looking for a van-based ice cream salesman.

'Which one shall I take?' I asked.

But she was adamant. 'Please come back tomorrow and I will find something more appropriate.'

Her distress at being unable to help me was quite touching, so I left empty-handed.

Two days later, I had four replies to my letters, one of which, from H.R. Howard and Sons in Ashton, upset me. It thanked me for my application but said that I was overqualified for the post and that they would be unable to hold me for long. When one needs work urgently any refusal hurts.

Another reply, from builders' merchants Samuel Gratrix, offered me an immediate interview.

I went there the following morning and met Mr Slater, manager of the glass department. The interview was quite formal, and he told me that he had several applicants for the job. The next morning another letter from him asked me to return for a second interview. I was offered the post immediately. He told me the salary, hours of work, and what the job entailed.

'When can you start work?' he asked.

'Tomorrow morning.'

Within a few days of walking away from P.J. Hillman, I was working again and Joan could leave her temporary job on the production line. I vowed that if she ever wished to start work again at some time in the future, it would be as a chiropodist, something for which she was qualified and really enjoyed.

Gratrix was based in Failsworth, about 300 yards from the famous Failsworth Pole, the site of an ancient maypole and now a landmark clock tower. The company supplied goods to the building industry — just about everything required to build and equip an entire house. The glass department provided metal windows, plain glass and figured glass in all sizes and weights to fill them, putty to bed them in, Insulight blocks, glazing bars, armour-plated doors, mirrors, splashbacks. You name it, they sold it.

Though house builders were the primary customers, anyone could call in for bits and pieces at the showrooms, so we took turns to ensure someone always manned the counter. My main job was to deal with people on the phone and supply their needs.

I had been working for just two hours when a telephone request came in for a large sheet of quarter-inch plate glass to replace a shop window. As I was writing down the dimensions, Mr Slater pushed a chart before me and pointed to the heavier glass needed for that size, which I dutifully explained to the shop owner. He became furious, and accused me of trying to sell him a more expensive item than he wanted. I was forced to accept his order on the understanding that it was against our advice. The glass was cut to his specifications, delivered and installed — and lasted just two days before cracking because his shop front was on a busy road with heavy vehicles passing only yards away. He telephoned and asked for me by name to apologise for doubting me, and requested a replacement in the correct weight. I never told him that his was the first order for glass that I had ever taken in my life and that I had merely followed the guide on a chart.

There was a lot to do, but I found the job easy and the hours manageable compared to what I had left. After Hillman's it almost felt like a holiday, and gave me more time at home with the family. I was also able to clear my mind, return to eating regularly and regain some of my weight loss. Joan visibly relaxed. She told me how worried she had been while I worked for Hillman, and expressed her relief that that episode was over.

But looking back on those years, it was not all doom and gloom. What had I gained? I had successfully completed an intensive business degree, I had undertaken driving lessons and a driving test with a free vehicle, and I was now equipped to face any challenge.

Joan had refused to consent when I mentioned that I could still accept the job offered by one of Harry's business customers. She said that it would be a return to the same kind of life, so I dropped that idea.

After three weeks in my new job, I received a letter from Harry asking if I would return. I was surprised by the letter, but not as surprised as what fell out of the envelope: a cheque for £200. The letter explained that the money was offered unconditionally. It was the first 'extra' he had ever given me. With the uncertainty over the new job, a young family to support, and an old house to maintain, the money was certainly welcome. I telephoned to thank him for the cheque, but also to confirm that I was not returning. I promised to call in to his new premises sometime in the near future. This I did several weeks later, and found the company struggling. Work demands meant that Harry and his wife could never be away from the office together, and they could not keep any of my replacements. Their first recruit was a qualified accountant who managed the first week satisfactorily, but then discovered that his duties constituted only part of what I had been doing, so he walked away with the comment that any more would be impossible. The next one lasted 10 days. His parting comment was that you would have to be crazy to work at that pace. It meant that Harry had to personally take on more of my work than he could handle; his wife Mary said that he would never live long enough to enjoy retirement.

P.J. Hillman gradually went downhill. Two ailing customers went out of business owing them money, leaving Harry to take over one in Leek and the other in Congleton, but neither could be salvaged when the parent company itself was having difficulties. Van drivers came and went because I had been filling in and covering deliveries. Finally, no one was checking that the vehicles were properly maintained or serviced, with consequent breakdowns and flat tyres.

About four years after I left, Harry arrived at his office very late one day, and dictated his will to his secretary, Winifred. After it was signed and witnessed, he said, 'Don't tell Mary, please send it to my accountants.'

He returned home and died later that day, aged about 53.

Joan later commented that had I stayed working for Hillman I would have suffered the same fate. When I think back now (with sorrow), I know that it would have been impossible to change him. He left enough in his will to make

Mary a wealthy widow with a superb house in Bramhall and huge valuable quantities of embroidery and guipure (lace).

There is an extraordinary postscript to my P.J. Hillman days, but I will return to it later.

Meanwhile, my time at Gratrix did not pass without incident, accident, or my usual habit of making an impact on whatever I did.

Mr Slater apologised one day for being short-staffed.

I laughed and said, 'We are not short-staffed; in fact I think one of us should be based at the sharp end where all the real work is being done, down in the workshop. I think Don is bored in this office and would be happier in the glass warehouse, organising the flow.'

Don was delighted to occupy a small room downstairs from where he was in sole charge of a single but vital operation, and was welcomed there as an asset.

Apparently, eight staff had been previously considered as a normal complement, but I felt that even six were not needed. My next suggestion came as a pleasant surprise to Max, one of the office staff. He was a friendly and personable young man who was also a scratch golfer.

I said to Mr Slater, 'Max should be out selling our business because he would do well, especially on the golf course.'

That move proved valuable to both Max and to Gratrix, and he was happier at work.

I spent some time in the workshop to better understand the operation — what products they handled, and the kind of problems encountered during a working day. They were co-operative and helpful when they learned that I was interested to learn and had their welfare at heart, especially when accepting orders and delivery schedules.

Several office departments occupied one very large room and tended to get in each other's way, especially when they all had to use the Banda Room at the far end. Everyone grumbled about it, yet nothing was ever done to improve matters. One very busy day I marched down to the boardroom, knocked on the door and just walked in to a full board meeting in progress.

To a silenced room, I said, 'Something needs sorting out urgently when you are free Mr Madden, but I apologise for the interruption.'

About an hour later, Mr Madden, the M.D., stood before me and very politely said, 'I believe you have a problem, Mr Cribb. How can I help?'

'May I apologise once more; had I known there was a meeting in progress, I would not have walked in. But if you turn and face the crowded room you may understand how difficult it can be to work efficiently without arguments.'

He turned and looked around for a few moments, and said, 'Yes, you have a point; I will deal with it, and thank you for bringing it to my notice.'

Within an hour, a team of men arrived and moved a group of about 14 along with their tables and desks out of the room, and made space for the remainder just as quickly. I never discovered where they were relocated, but everyone else seemed delighted.

A voice in the room said, 'Who the hell is that chap? He's not been here ten minutes and gets something done we've been complaining about for ages.' I recognised that voice as coming from someone who complained about everything.

Once I understood precisely how all the systems worked, I began targeting metal windows as a key product, guessing that other sales would automatically follow, a judgement that was to prove correct. It was a fascinating, challenging and ultimately lucrative mathematical process of combining different sizes bolted together to fit almost any required window dimension commonly in use. The trick lay in finding the minimum number of units needed to produce the maximum number of frame sizes then estimating whether to multiply that quantity by two or more to hold in stock. The last bit took longer but after several calls to our house-builder customers, it began to fall into place.

Builders were installing metal windows in many new houses, and we supplied one that our customers seemed to prefer, Crittalls Metal Windows. My next step was to get manufacturers to understand that supply must be reliable and promises kept once delivery dates had been agreed. I made it very clear that no wild promises would be accepted by our customers. Builders were happy to work around given dates just so they knew when to expect supplies.

One particular builder got used to ringing me direct to supply other materials not connected with our department. I was once again forced to see the M.D. who said that the builder had already spoken to him and that he had issued instructions to all departments that they had to accept orders through me because the customer was so important.

Sales from the glass department soared, followed by everything else that went into new homes, so I was always chasing up not just our own deliveries but also those from all other areas. I never had a problem with anyone else because sales were improving, Mr Madden was satisfied, and metal windows were leading the way.

With improved sales, there is always a price to pay. I would regularly check that every promised delivery was actually on the wagon before it left our depot. I often reached the loading bay via the goods hoist. On one occasion I did not notice a heavy radiator standing in the hoist, and when the hoist jerked to a stop the radiator fell on to my heel. The pain was so bad that I was afraid to look down because I thought my foot had gone. Several loaders rushed over when they heard the crash.

I handed one a delivery note, and said, 'Will you please make sure all these are loaded first.'

They were astonished

One said, 'Get your priorities right, you've injured your leg.'

But I insisted he got the supplies loaded first.

When my shoe was removed the foot swelled up immediately. Someone drove me to Oldham Hospital, where an X-ray showed that no bones were broken, so it was strapped up firmly and an ambulance arranged to take me home.

But I was having none of it. 'Would you please phone Gratrix and ask if someone will take me back to work.'

The staff were incredulous, but complied. When I got back to work, no one could believe that I preferred to carry on working.

One said, 'You're entitled to claim compensation because that radiator should not have been left there, and any sensible person would have several weeks off with pay.'

That's not my style. I hobbled about, hopped up and down stairs and later got the bus home. I refused to allow my limbs or my brain to seize up just sitting about doing nothing. Several people tried to persuade me to make a claim, but apart from allowing an entry to be written in the accident book, I refused to take the matter any further.

Out of the blue, one day in our showroom I bumped into a friend from my old digs, the Manor House in Oldham: Darrell Shaw. He did not know that I worked there, but assumed that, like him, I was a customer looking for something.

'Why are you wasting your time here,' he said, 'when you should be doing a more responsible job? I'll be in touch with you soon.'

Within a week I had a letter from him saying that L. Spinners needed a group quality control manager for all their mills, and would I be interested. I phoned him to say that it was not my kind of job and he sounded relieved. I gathered he had something else in mind for me and guessed that the group had asked him to make the offer.

Darrell contacted me again shortly after, and asked me to visit him on a Saturday morning at Park Mill in Royton.

He seemed distracted when I arrived.

I said, 'If it's not convenient for you, it's okay, I can come another time.'

'No,' he said, 'it's just that I've forgotten something and will have to visit head office.'

Then, almost as an afterthought, he said, 'You can come with me if you want, it's not far.'

He drove to the company's head office. Initially the place seemed quiet, until he led me down a corridor, opened a door at the far end and we walked in to find several people sitting around a boardroom table. I was invited to sit down as he announced that I was being interviewed for a senior post with the group.

His shock tactic did not faze me at all, in fact I found it amusing, especially when I was faced by a couple of familiar faces — one a former director from Joshua Hoyle, now their new M.D., Clifford Cummings, and another who was the brother of the late Clara Bracewell. Together with his own cousin, Edward Garfield, and the company secretary, they were the five executive directors of the company.

They gave me a good grilling, with Darrell being the most incisive, placing specific problems before me and asking what my solutions would be in the face of opposition by others.

I found it interesting and enjoyable, and sensed that Darrell was deliberately testing me to prove my suitability to the others. Knowing Harry Hillman from the Manor House days gave Darrell the certainty that anyone who worked with that difficult and demanding person must have needed special qualities — and equipped me to manage anything they might want. In a nutshell, they were looking for someone to turn a loss-making unit into a profitable one.

When all of them appeared to be satisfied, Clifford Cummings cleared his throat and spoke in his familiar slow, carefully modulated tones.

'We are prepared to offer you the post of manager at Park Mill at the starting salary of a thousand pounds, and after six months increase it to fifteen hundred if you prove satisfactory. Other allowances and expenses will be discussed between Darrel and yourself. We can also offer you a house in Chadderton, which we had intended to sell, but if you become part of our organisation you may either rent or buy it.'

My immediate thought was that within six months I would have trebled my current income, with a house on top. But my reply surprised them.

'Thank you for the offer, but before accepting it may I first ask some questions. I do not know much about your group, or what your future policies are, so please tell me something about your history and your future intentions.'

When I heard them out, it seemed satisfactory, at least in theory, and my next statement surprised them even more.

'May I look around the mill and make an assessment before giving you my final answer.'

Darrell and I returned to the mill. We walked up the steps into the newly equipped and 'modernised' textile operation. But I needed only five minutes to see that the 'new' machinery was nothing more than the same old machines simply regrouped and combined into continuous feed units. To an untrained eye it may have appeared satisfactory, but my heart was heavy with apprehension. I had worked on textile machinery as good or better in India many years earlier. To make things more complicated, this plant did not produce conventional cotton yarns but something called 'condenser' yarns, not just new to me but apparently to everyone else in the group. It looked weak, uneven and full of faults.

I said to Darrell, 'It will take three years for this unit to become profitable — and that is just an estimate.'

He accepted my analysis of the factory's prospects.

Then it was time to see the house they offered. I took Joan to see 83 Birch Avenue, just the two of us. I turned the key in the door and we stepped inside.

Before we had even opened another door, Joan looked at me and said, 'Can we buy it, please.'

We both instantly felt the house was right for both of us.

'Yes,' I said, 'we will buy it.'

That house, combined with a much better income, was the clincher, even though I knew the new business had a mountain to climb. I owed it not just to my wife but also to my three children. I accepted the offer to start work in October 1963.

Like most things that happened to me, my move from one job to the next did not go smoothly.

36

TWENTY-YEAR STINT

Handing in my notice at Gratrix produced more activity than anticipated. Mr Slater asked me to wait until he had seen the M.D.

On his return he said, 'I have been given the authority to tell you that when I retire later this year you can take my place as manager of this department. If you stay, you will get a substantial increase immediately, which will be raised again when I retire. Since your arrival, turnover has more than trebled and you deserve to be treated accordingly.'

Why, I thought, does this only happen when I propose to leave, and when I have already given my word to take up another post? Despite building some close connections over the previous nine months, I didn't want to break a promise to Darrell. Plus a better 'nest' beckoned for my family, so I had to decline, once again with a slight feeling of guilt for my relatively short stay. I explained to Mr Slater about the importance of a new home. He understood just how much that mattered, and stressed how sorry he was to see me leave.

That final week went by very quickly because I did everything possible to leave a clear map of where the business stood. However, my last Friday was painful, and I mean physically painful. I was doubled up with a mysterious stomach ache. Colleagues who saw me bent double then straighten up wondered what I was doing. By the time I got home I felt really ill.

After I went to the toilet, Joan asked, 'How long have you been passing blood?'

She immediately sent for Dr Paton, our GP, who in turn called for an ambulance to take me to Westhulme Isolation Hospital in Oldham where medics took samples of my diarrhoea. Meanwhile, I couldn't keep anything down, even drinking water kept coming back. They brought a tube.

I asked, 'What's that for?'

'To feed water down your throat,' said the nurse, 'without liquid you will suffer dehydration.'

'No,' I said, 'give me a cup and a teaspoon and I will make it stay down. I don't want a tube in my throat.'

But even a small spoonful wouldn't stay down.

'Please let me carry on,' I said, 'I will get it to work.'

At first, I just wet the spoon and licked it, then took a few drops which stayed down and very gradually increased it until I could manage a teaspoonful, after which I was able to sip water from the cup and slowly increase the quantity. Fifteen minutes later I was able to drink a whole cupful without trouble.

Sister watched with interest. 'You are a very determined young man,' she said, 'I didn't think it was possible, but you did it. Now you have to swallow a lot of salt and water and take these tablets. Drink it all and we'll get some more.'

She came back with a hypodermic syringe and took my arm.

I said, 'Do you mind if I faint?'

'Don't you dare,' she retorted sharply.

I could see the young medic behind her grinning at me. He knew I was winding her up.

I continued to drink countless jugfuls of salty water and take more tablets to replace lost minerals. Worryingly, their tests proceeded with no conclusive results. I continued passing diarrhoea and blood for another five days before it stopped. They never found the cause during the week I was in hospital (or ever). Nevertheless, I had lost a lot of weight.

I returned home to Joan, weak but still cheerful, to be informed that Dr Paton had visited her in my absence.

'Knowing your husband, he will want to start work immediately but it is too dangerous in his state,' he had told her. 'That is why I am avoiding him. He must rest at home for at least three weeks and I will return to see then if he is strong enough.'

I received a letter from Darrell Shaw warning me against starting work too soon, and a week later my first four-weekly salary payment arrived. Apparently the company always paid two weeks in advance and two behind, so I had been paid my first salary without even going through the door.

I began work the following month, although I was still building up my strength. The first few weeks were spent getting the feel of the place and the people, looking at records of machine installations, and familiarising myself with suppliers of raw materials. If I had been concerned before, my scrutiny of the works reinforced my worries. I was under no illusion that I had taken on an immense job.

By this stage of my life I had enough experience of various facets of business to take on this challenge while remaining clear-sighted about how hard things might become. The Lancashire textile industry was steadily contracting and everyone in it – even if they were blessed with the best equipment – was swimming against the tide. I also still had the same strong instincts that shaped my approach during my Bombay days. If I was going to help Park Mill succeed, it would involve working from the bottom up. This meant close involvement with the production process and infrastructure. It also meant being habitually wary of delays and indecisions that came from board level, from those who were much more than 'arm's length' away from the factory floor. Over time, both to my satisfaction and frustration, these instincts would prove to be a reliable guide.

The building had lain empty for four years without any heating or maintenance. Consequently, there were some worrying signs of dilapidation: ceilings were cracked and flaking where iron in the reinforced concrete had rusted, windows on most floor levels had rotten wooden frames, and the main roof leaked.

Understandably, the workforce were suspicious of a new manager, especially one who asked questions about everything that should seem obvious to anyone growing up in the textile industry. I did not fit into their picture of a traditional manager, or indeed fit into any familiar category. They kept their reservations to themselves, but I could sense their reluctance to be forthcoming. When they eventually came round, I was told that no former manager had ever spoken directly to anyone, but only communicated through their supervisors.

It was not only the shop floor that was unsettled: the winding-room manager made it clear that I had taken the job he should have been given. He would have made a sound, traditional manager, but the place needed someone with more skills and imagination to survive. He did not conceal his feelings or his contempt for this soft, new arrival, but I decided to wait my time before making any move to disillusion him.

The first major decision I made at Park Mill was to have all the machine parts lying around the room collected and listed. The installers had moved out and left surplus spares where they lay, so I found all their invoices at head office and worked out their cash value, which amounted to several thousand pounds. I was fortunate to have a visit from one of the company's local service engineers at that moment, who told me that his CEO — a difficult man, feared by his minions — would be abroad for two or three weeks on business. I decided to use this information to my advantage.

I listed each item with its value on an invoice, then I added my own (implied) version of our agreement in a letter. I said that if these parts were not collected immediately and a cheque for their value not received before their chief returned, he would be furious. It worked like a charm and I knew that they would never bother him with trifling details like correctly completing a contract.

My first three months was time well spent learning about raw material suppliers, and how they operated. They were impressed by the depth of my inquiries, but for my part I really needed to get to grips with something new to me.

Spinning of waste materials (shorter fibres extracted from conventional spinning processes) was described to me as more of an art than a science, but I was later to think that it would need a bit of magic arts as well. In a nutshell, we were using raw material that was too cheap, producing yarn that was poor quality, which created a high percentage of waste, and most importantly gave the spinners a workload that was unsustainable.

One day I challenged Darrell and practically demanded control of raw material purchases, not realising that it was exclusively the domain of company directors. But my insistence eventually paid off, and I began buying only the best available. The result? A rise in production, happier spinners, less waste, fewer 'seconds', and an increase in sales.

Darrell then insisted that we speed up the machines by 10% to further increase production. I was unable to stop him. From the outset it was a disastrous move, undoing all we had achieved. Many people were almost in tears at the extra work and threatened to walk out, so without further reference to him we returned everything to their former levels.

That was not the first or last time he made changes against my advice, which later had to be reversed. Some of it proved costly. The man himself was always polite and gentlemanly, and we remained friendly and on good terms, but I often asked him to leave the problems to me so that they could be solved satisfactorily. He obliged most of the time.

Darrell was useful in other ways. He exploited old school contacts that introduced new business outlets. Unfortunately, retaining those openings often proved difficult when customers were naturally interested only in products that would be profitable.

So much was to happen in those 20 years that a short summary might be helpful and allow details to emerge as I proceed.

Even though the business started as a spinning mill, it would, over time, become an industrial complex sustaining wholly owned and part-owned subsidiaries. Their emergence would have been impossible without a suitable building in which a functioning operation already existed. The importance of 'surviving' long enough to allow start-up businesses to become profitable without expensive overheads cannot be underestimated, and my key role was to help us to keep going. This was no easy matter, especially after a big fire in 1970.

However, before all that took place, we had a battle to find suitable markets. There were many issues to address, including modifying production several times, and relying on the wonderful employees to work long hours without compensation. I often worked beside them doing precisely what they did to prove that I could keep pace with their work rate.

Good staff were key to a successful operation, but not all made the cut, and I was forced to weed out lazy or uncooperative people. I also found it necessary to break company rules (which often put me in the M.D.'s bad books), and promote good employees to responsible positions. Worse, from the viewpoint of senior staff, I took on at least one young person every year from corrective institutions and almost begged everyone to give them a chance by encouraging and helping them. Incredibly, we only had three failures (including one case where I was fortunate not to be beaten up), but many success stories. One or two left to start their own business ventures, and thanked me for giving them a leg up.

Even though most of my time was taken up at work, I must end this chapter back at 83 Birch Avenue. Soon after starting work, I asked to see the company solicitor who told me that the house had already been signed over to me (prior to our first visit) at a price marginally below market value.

He said, 'They must trust and value you to do it without any money changing hands, as a welcome to your new abode.'

That single act ensured my loyalty because it meant so much to Joan. It became her haven, her cosy love nest, and her desire to remain as a full-time wife and mother. She never wanted to move away. After those first 10 years it must have felt wonderful for her to have a home with all mod cons and an income that allowed more than basic living.

37

TERRITORIAL INFLUENCE

After all my endeavours to make the place profitable, reduce labour turnover to a historic low, and make myself available at all times, who could imagine what could happen next. Despite always being willing to accept whatever life threw at me, what happened next shocked even me.

After spending two weeks in bed with a high temperature, the phone rang and an unfamiliar voice asked if I was fit enough to come in to work for a meeting with him and all the staff. I crawled out of bed and arrived there to meet WPC, a new employee appointed by Edwin Garfield to run the business over my head. He was announced as the 'saviour' of the industry, 'the best man ever available', and I was to assist him in every way because he now assumed all my former responsibilities. There had been no warnings about his emergence, no contact with me by Edwin, no explanations, just his sudden appearance. Darrell was away (probably avoiding me), but after my severe bout of influenza I remained passive. Really, I was in no state to object. It turned out that WPC had wanted my presence at the meeting as a sort of tacit approval. After the meeting I returned home to bed.

It took about another two weeks after my return to discover that he knew absolutely nothing about our business, even less about business in general, and had no idea how to manage a workforce or understand what made them tick. One thing he did have were lofty ideas about his own importance and how he deserved special treatment. He had been awarded a luxury car, a splendid salary, and a free hand to claim enormous expenses, which he did from the start. This was the man who was now buying all our raw material with the full consent of the board. It was all an utter mystery to me.

The first thing he discussed with me was Roy Gillespie, our sales manager.

'We have to get rid of him,' he said, 'he has to go.'

'Over my dead body,' was my immediate response. 'If he goes, so do I.'

He was taken aback by my response, and quickly let it drop, because without me he would have been unable to cope, and he knew it.

There is no point labouring details about the following months (or longer) when I had to carry this useless person, during which time it is worth mentioning the lack of response from Darrell, which surprised me. He appeared to accept the appointment with typical public school stiff upper lip, polite demeanour, and stand-offishness — baffling for normal human beings, but I was getting tired of baling out the ship as it wallowed and became more difficult to maintain on course. I stayed out of loyalty to all those people who had helped to build and maintain a profitable concern, but my patience with the board of directors was wearing thin. Were they blind, I wondered, or more stupid than I thought possible?

Then one day it all got too much and decided I had to go. I began filling two empty cartons with documents that I did not wish to leave behind, with the intention of burning them. Darrell walked in.

'What are you doing?' he asked.

'Leaving a sinking ship,' I said. 'I've had enough.'

I could see he was concerned, even a little shocked.

'Just hang on for another half-hour,' he said, 'I'm going to head office and will be back soon.'

Twenty minutes later, he returned, walked into the boardroom, and emerged five minutes later with WPC, who immediately left the premises and never came back. He had been dismissed on the spot. Darrell said that when it came to a choice, he could not afford to lose me. He never told me what he had said to Edwin. I never asked.

Then Edwin appeared and I was ushered into the boardroom with both of them. The M.D. coloured up and apologised for what had happened, then confessed that the departed man had been his C.O. in the Territorial Army and had 'informed him' of his super credentials for the job, and 'naturally one must accept these things from another public school type without question' (my words, not his). He actually asked me to forgive him.

My great relief at the sudden turn of events and departure of 'dead wood' completely wiped out everything else from my mind. It was only much later that I realised how very slow I had been to capitalise on an ideal opportunity to enhance my pay and conditions by simply requesting the money saved by his departure. On reflection I knew that I would not have done that — it just wasn't me — but I could have joked about it. Joan was so correct in once more calling me 'slow John Ridd'.

Michael, my first raw material supplier, hung his head when he called, and apologised for never asking to see me, even as a friendly visitor. Then he told me why he could not. Apparently, he had been a regular supplier to a company run by WPC's uncle, and knew all about him.

'I had to avoid contact with you because I could not reveal what I knew about him,' said Michael. 'His uncle would not trust him to even buy one bale of cotton or to do anything of importance in his place. We were all surprised to see him here instead of you, but accepted it because he carried on buying from us.'

'How successful was the business,' I asked, 'was it large?'

He laughed. 'It would have fitted into your cellar.'

Other suppliers confirmed what Michael said, and agreed that it had been an easy ride for them during his tenancy because he accepted everything offered by raw material salesmen without question. Now they expressed relief at 'getting me back' at the helm.

However, I was now faced with additional problems managing two 'new' acrylic plants on floors two and three. A wonderful set of patient, hardworking and experienced spinners attempting to produce saleable yarn on inappropriate machines was never going to work. We soldiered on, but after 18 months of dealing with irate customers and too many returns, we were forced to give up. I remember Edwin asking me at a meeting why I had bought unsuitable machines and I referred him to his cousin sitting beside him for the answer.

His next question was, 'Why did you not get them brought up to date by machinery experts?'

This time I was ready, so I handed out two letters from the experts I had consulted. Both stated that it would cost more to update them than buy new machinery, and even then we would be left with inappropriate machines for the job.

Darrell decided to sell the machines, but I laughed at the idea.

'Who,' I asked, 'would buy a load of junk?'

He persisted and brought in some potential customers. They looked down the lines and walked out without a word. The next one did not go beyond the door, laughed, turned around and we distinctly heard mention of 'a load of scrap'.

'Okay,' he said, 'scrap the lot.'

What a waste of time and money it had all been — and this was only one of numerous occasions when similar decisions were taken against advice from me and others closer to the sharp end. Buying 'cheap' rather than sensible often resulted in wasted time and money, both vital commodities.

38

STAYING ON

It had always been my intention not to remain in one job for too long — not to get into a rut, become complacent, or become 'part of the furniture'.

For many reasons the post at Park Mill was destined to hold me much longer. The reasons? Gratitude for our new home in a quiet suburb with a good school close by for my children, loyalty to my long-time friend Darrell, my desire to keep a promise, my responsibility to the workforce, and a view that I was actually able to help keep the mill alive and healthy.

During this time I was offered several other jobs, although I never mentioned them to anyone else. The first one arrived in May or June 1964 when a visitor asked for me by name. He announced that finding me had been difficult and that he had been commissioned by my previous M.D. at Gratrix to offer me a job with the company to which he had moved. Apparently, he had been influenced by a large builder I had serviced who said he should get me back as his main contact and to offer me really good terms and conditions. When I thanked him and declined his offer, the emissary was stunned. Eventually he had to accept that I kept my promises and would not leave until I had turned loss into profit.

The next offer came from a rival company via two people who had been asked to find the best man to fill a vacancy for a key senior post. They both saw me on the same day, one in the morning and the other in the afternoon. By this time I had been doing my job for at least five years, and although the business was now profitable we had to implement important changes to make our product more saleable. I believed that I was the best innovator they had, so felt compelled to soldier on. Again I declined a really good offer.

The biggest financial offer came from a large, well-known consultancy that spent several months within the group. I became good friends with their senior executive. We worked together for long periods, had lunches together and sometimes went to the local swimming pool during lunch breaks. He was a strong and active man who had played rugby for Scotland and treated me like he would other rugger players and expected me to take everything he dished out.

One day he said, 'You are exactly the type of person we need, and we would be happy if you could join the firm. Your income would triple immediately with bonuses added over time.'

I said, 'Thank you, John, but I feel sure there will be snags. You have been in this area for several months now so obviously much of your life has to be spent away from home, and I am not prepared to leave my wife and family for long periods. I will discuss it with Joan, but I already know how she feels.'

When I told Joan of the offer, stressing the huge increase in income, she smiled and said, 'Would you really like to accept the job? I won't stop you if it makes you happy.'

So I changed tack and countered with, 'Would you like a different lifestyle or a bigger house?'

'I already have everything I need now,' she said, and then with one of her impish grins, added, 'as long as I have you.'

I apologised to John for rejecting his offer and thanked him for making it. He was expecting my refusal after our previous discussion, but said he wanted to leave the offer open. At that stage I wasn't aware that his CEO was on his way to see me. Apparently, he left recruitment in the hands of senior staff, but occasionally came as back-up to help convince reluctant prospects like me. I met him, listened politely and expressed real regret at being unable to join the group, where, I told him, I would have enjoyed every new challenge offered — but only as a single man.

Another really interesting offer came from a much larger textile company, once again through a third party. Even though the salary proposed was excellent I had no wish to become a cog, even an important one, in a huge machine. A friend who had been with them before setting up on his own, advised me against the offer.

He said, 'Bill, you will hate the inflexibility, infighting, and the sheer number of fools you will have to suffer. It is not you, because you often bend or break rules to benefit the company. They will never accept mavericks, even if it saves them huge amounts of money.'

He told me that he sometimes booked his own flights at considerable savings, yet was chastised for not using their own (very inefficient) travel department.

Despite all the offers, I stayed on at Park Mill.

Returning to personnel problems, there was one incident with the manager of the winding department, Norman (who believed I had usurped his job), when I was forced to act. He was deliberately rude to me in full view of his charges and I quietly asked him to step into his office where I shut the door.

'To show respect for you before your workforce, I refrained from retaliating in public, but I must warn you now that should it ever happen again I will not hesitate to tear you apart in front of them. I really have no wish to do that but I will if necessary.'

I walked out without another word.

He became a changed man from that day and I won brownie points from his winders for my restraint and not showing him up. Norman proved to be an asset and became a work friend right up to his retirement.

Our office manager, Olive, was another I hoped to win over as an ally, but it nearly became a disaster when I walked into the office one morning carrying a heavy ledger.

'I am fed up with their requests,' she said, 'always wanting something when they come to the office window.'

I flung the ledger across the room where it landed with a loud bang, which silenced the office.

I said, 'They are the ones who do all the hard work, and without them we would not have a job. We are here to look after their interests and be grateful that we do not have to work long hours in the kind of conditions they have to endure.'

Then this middle-aged, old-fashioned woman surprised me.

She said, 'I never thought about it like that before. Thank you Mr Cribb, I've learned something I will never forget.'

Not only did she mean it, but she almost began recruiting me in order to help those she described as 'the poor man who has to push all that weight about' or 'the lad in the cellar on such a pathetic wage'. She became a much happier and more understanding person.

There was another reason I needed her support. I had a plan to reduce about 27 wage scales to around 15 by raising the lowest paid very gradually. One word from Olive to head office could have scuppered my plans. I started the slow process by seeing each individual myself, telling them that if word got out to anyone it would be seen as a mistake and their wage would revert to their lower rate. Over three years, not a single person ever discussed it. Olive became a willing confidant and maintained a diplomatic silence about it, almost hugging it to herself with great joy.

Running that place encouraged me to support all the hard work that produced profits for the company, but it also forced me to be tougher with shirkers and cheats. I needed only the best people. The first to go was the 'engineer', one who had been promoted because he had impressed DHS by almost crawling to fulfil his every whim. He had been turning the boiler off over the weekends to save fuel oil, which was creating havoc, especially in winter, where cold machinery took all day to warm up and would run so badly that spinners were finding excuses to stay away on Monday mornings. I ordered him to keep it running seven days a week and he complained to my director that I would be wasting money. I won — and production, as expected, went up.

He did so many crazy things. Asked to put both compressors in action, he complied but arranged it so that they worked in opposition to each other. On another occasion he borrowed three men for a whole day to mount a shaft across two beams and only discovered at the moment of lift that it was two feet short — he had failed to measure the gap. What gave me the opportunity to terminate the employment of this impossible man was that I found he was robbing the company — buying raw materials to make wrought iron gates for his personal customers. He even bought all the special tooling equipment he needed for his 'moonlighting'. I picked my moment and walked into the workshop when he was working on some partly finished gates. I challenged him and asked him to leave the premises. He blustered and threatened to contact his union, so I offered to do it for him. He left immediately, taking all the equipment with him. I said, 'Good riddance and cheaply done.'

More than balancing out the poor employees, we had some stars. I asked the electrician, Roy, to take over as chief engineer because he was not only a highly qualified electrical engineer but also a very practical and sensible person. We were fortunate in having someone like him in situ. He was so trustworthy that I broke another company rule and told him that he could set his own work timetables. It created a storm with the board of directors, but I refused to budge. My next hurdle was getting him proper staff conditions and pay. Darrell said that making Roy a member of staff would satisfy his ego and that he would not be concerned with income. I shook my head in disbelief and agreed to see Roy about it. As an employer, we were still lost in the past.

'What do you consider as more important,' I asked him, 'staff status or a bigger income?'

'Bugger the status,' he replied, 'just give me the money!'

I reported back, saying at the same time that he should get both status and a better income because he was worth it. I got my way. He proved over the years to be the best employee we had and easily the most competent engineer in the group. He also became a good friend to me in every way even though, despite my protests, he always addressed me as 'Mr Cribb', even away from the workplace.

The control units originally supplied with the new machinery were not satisfactory, so Roy asked me if he could devise a better one. In time he came up with a greatly improved system and with my approval changed all the existing units to match. His capacity for innovation and his thinking outside the box matched up with how I operated; our teamwork was one vital element in helping to make Park successful.

Roy Gillespie, the sales manager, was another who worked very hard to satisfy customers' wishes, never concerned about how often he had to travel back and forth. He would ask us for minor modifications — 'a bit softer', or 'more strength' or 'less twist', and we would experiment endlessly to satisfy their requirements, succeeding more often than not. One or two customers said that it was good to have a supplier that cared enough to work with them so willingly. R.G. must take most of the credit for that.

Roy Fitton was also instrumental in helping to build and commission our conditioning chamber in the cellar, in which we fitted waterproof lighting that could withstand 100 degree temperatures and 100% relative humidity. The chamber was covered in special paint able to withstand raging conditions and had safety fridge handles fitted inside both doors for safe escape from the air-tight room.

With a good team of machine fitters led by Jack Fox, we were able to maintain everything by routine servicing. Jack could see almost instinctively if modifications would help. It was just unfortunate that the machinery was so imprecise and old-fashioned, but we were stuck with it.

Perhaps I ought to mention that every mill that started out with the same machinery — and there were many — scrapped everything within the first year or two because they could not get it to produce decent yarn. Two mills in the USA scrapped everything after one year. It took innovation, imagination, perseverance, a wonderful workforce, and sheer determination to run them profitably.

In 1970 life at work suddenly became so difficult that I thought we were finished. Just when everything was moving forward, slowly but satisfactorily, and during a fortnight when I was taking a break after having spent 'Wakes Weeks' holding the fort while everyone was away, we had a fire. A real, big, bad fire that threatened to finish the building. The damage was so extensive that, understandably, the board of directors wanted to retain the massive insurance payments for the other mills in the group, proposing to shut down Park and sell the building with the site. It was a dark period. We had to put in very long hours, and it often felt as if we were starting again, but this time under conditions of radical uncertainty. Somehow, I am not sure how, we got through it.

39

TRYING TIMES

My sons Mike and Alan had by this stage progressed to Chadderton Grammar School for Boys just down the road from the house. Caroline was preparing to join the same grammar school for girls on Broadway. It would have been odd if three bright children had not been accepted, despite the fact that all three had in turn suffered from everything that children could possibly get when growing up. The boys had developed serious breathing problems. Mike also contracted brucellosis, a condition that was not diagnosed properly for a long time, and made life extremely difficult for him. Neither boy was able to take part in sport for most of their time at the school, but Alan eventually joined the basketball team and got a blue in his final year. Mike's heroic struggle to get fit came later, to which I will return. Caroline was diagnosed with glandular fever as her first grammar school term was about to start, which meant she was sent to the B stream where Spanish was taught, not French as in the A stream. She was stuck with a Spanish teacher that no one liked for the duration.

One day David Russell, senior chiropodist at Oldham Health Centre, arrived unexpectedly at number 83 to see Joan. He asked if she would be interested in returning to work part-time. He said that she could choose her own working hours and start with one session a week on a day of her choice.

We knew both David and his wife Alice very well, two likeable Scots in spite (or perhaps because) of Alice's outspoken nature. Once, during dinner at our home shortly after we were married, Alice said to Joan, 'Marriage has been good for you, and you are more relaxed than I have ever known you to be.'

I knew that removing Joan from under the shadow of her father had been the most important factor in her transformation, but she was a very private person so I said nothing.

We concluded that working from 10 a.m. to 1 p.m. every Monday would allow Joan to be at home when the children left for school and be there when they got back. She had an open invitation to add extra morning shifts when she was ready to do more. Joan later added another morning a week, then a couple of years later was happily working every morning. She enjoyed being in harness again, and her income helped to swell the family coffers. All her patients clamoured to have her as their regular chiropodist, but it was impossible to see all of them. I was fortunate that she was always mine.

Now I should return to a postscript to my time at P.J. Hillman. About a year after I had walked away from Harry, I was visited at home by the Manchester-based manager of London Life Insurance. The visit would make a significant impact on our income.

The manager told us that Harry had taken out a special pension scheme for me during my time with him. Although the premiums had not been paid since I left the company, the fund would be held with them until I retired at 65. As I write, in the last 23 years that tiny sum has been paying me £465 each year, an incredible return from the original £179 paid in by Harry. When London Life became part of AMP, they sent me an additional lump sum of £1,000!

However, the greatest benefit from his visit was far more valuable. He not only pointed out a need for investment, but also suggested a scheme known as a half-payment system — we paid half and they paid half. Our first policy was for £3,000. When he returned after two years, we paid the full premium, again for £3,000. We kept repeating that every time he returned until we had a string of policies running together. The returns were so good that two of the children also opened policies. Eventually government legislation disallowed their policies. I never understood why, because the policyholders were the main beneficiaries. Strung together, our policies returned enough capital to have bought another similar house outright.

Joan had always been keen on dancing but I was never able to dance with her, so one day I suggested that we went to Billingtons Dance Academy to learn some ballroom and Latin American steps from a professional. Starting in a large group of beginners, we progressed to having private lessons from Mrs Billington and kept up the lessons for five years, really enjoying ourselves and getting lots of exercise in the process. All three of our children wanted to do the same, but unlike their parents they formalised lessons by getting their bronze, silver and gold medals from the IDTA. I must add that they were all natural dancers and good movers. I was especially proud of Mike at this time. He had exercised regularly, and endured great setbacks for three or four years to get fit enough just to function normally. He showed enormous courage to keep going where I may have been ready to give up. His perseverance and sheer guts won my admiration. I will never forget his determination to go on and on, fighting to get his breath day after day and month after month until he succeeded. It was inspirational and unforgettable.

By 1970, we had added an extension to the rear of the house, built by Brian Parker, a builder who did a lot of work for us at the mill. I insisted that he give me a competitive price and that he would be paid after satisfying us that it was done properly. I believe he was grateful that I played it straight. Mike was finally able to have his own room in the extension, and for the first time all three children had rooms of their own.

I instigated a scheme at work where staff could use the facilities or trades people we used at the same prices available to the company — but it all had to be above board. Anyone found buying anything for personal use under the cover of company purchasing, would be dismissed, and this was checked by me every month when I passed all purchase invoices. It worked very well because everyone knew that it was necessary. I was the only person who broke company rules by buying without board permission, simply because awaiting decisions from board meetings would often lose bargains, vital machinery or plant that might have been snapped up by others. The appearance of these items on invoices placed before the M.D. always brought rebukes, sometimes explosions of anger, the most memorable being when I bought a forklift truck.

Permission had been given to buy a secondhand forklift for £7,500. I took advice from companies that used them about the purchase and they all advised that I would just be buying trouble for that price because repairs would cost a fortune on the outdated and inefficient machine. Everyone said, 'Buy a new one.' So I did, for £27,500.

The M.D. was furious, refusing to speak to me for being so rebellious. It was almost six months before he came round from head office to see me, by which time I had also put in a lift from the ground floor bale storage to the opening room to simplify the movement from unloading to transportation upstairs. It worked like a dream, saving three wages, increasing production, sales and profits.

I knew that he was curious about how this had happened, and I could see he was impressed when he saw it.

'Congratulations Bill,' he said, 'I can see now that you were right all along. It looks good and works well.'

'Not good enough,' I said, 'I want a physical pat on the back along with those words.'

I got one — and he blushed as he did it.

I broke so many rules, too numerous to mention, all done to push the pace along and make things happen, often with help from key players who also understood what was needed. With the aid of an expert machinery supplier and two men, we dismantled a doubling machine on the east coast, moved it into the works and had it re-erected and working over the space of one weekend. Before it was revealed on an invoice it was already boosting our weekly profits and stilled the voice of protest from H.Q. I always made sure that everyone was well paid for anything beyond their normal duties and hours, so I never had problems with recruits.

My habit of reading the financial pages every day, seeing every caller even for a few minutes to assess their market news value, and routinely evaluating how other businesses functioned, allowed me to sense how markets were moving across a wide spectrum. I can remember not buying raw material at all for a long time, which really worried DHS when he discovered we were selling short, a dangerous position. He berated me soundly.

'Don't worry,' I said, 'I've got it in hand.'

He glared at me and walked out.

Good offers trickled in from our suppliers over the next three days and I pretended to agree, reluctantly, to buy vast quantities from four of them 'as a favour because they were good dealers'.

Darrell banged down their contracts on my desk and bellowed, 'What the hell are you playing at now, going over the top and flooding us with raw material. We're manufacturers, not cotton merchants.' Then he slammed out.

I was so lucky, because prices began rising steadily for three weeks, then doubled, and continued rising further. Darrel said, 'Why didn't you buy more?'

My reply to him is unprintable.

Those purchases helped us keep important customers because I suggested to our sales manager that we average down prices by combining their remaining contracts with new ones in order to help their own sales. They were grateful for our help because it would have been very difficult for them to sell at the new market prices. I asked Roy not to discuss our plan with the directors as he wanted to do.

My open door policy at work resulted in visitors getting to know several of our employees, who were free to walk in whenever they had problems. Visiting directors or M.D.s also enjoyed the atmosphere. Fortunately, most employees were able to sense when to walk out again, so it worked well. However, the policy encouraged some moments of humour, like the time when a dozen women stormed in, all angrily shouting at the same time, and I leaned back in my chair and laughed aloud. After a short silence, one asked why I was laughing.

I said, 'Come and sit in my chair and look at what I can see and hear.'

They settled down, and I said, 'Two of you sit down and the rest go back to work.'

We were soon able to resolve their problem quite easily.

Everyone at work knew that I was definitely a 'one-off'; they only had to look at the car I drove — an old black Ford Popular, a car that staff described as 'the worst car in the place'. It had cost me £50, and another £50 to make it roadworthy. It served me well for two years. My sons were so embarrassed that they begged me to drop them well away from the school gates and never to take them inside the grounds.

Following the disaster with the acrylic plants, I began pushing for modern, precision-built textile machinery only available in Germany, Switzerland and Italy. Darrell met my suggestion with derision.

'We can't afford it, so forget it,' he said.

'Then shut the place now,' I said. 'Without modernisation we can't survive much longer. We have too many people producing too little on old machinery; it will eventually kill us. Additionally, we have a wholly owned subsidiary managed by a very competent M.D. now developing successfully, so we need to keep this place alive and pay our proportion of costs until that business is large enough to survive without our support.'

The company that I was referring to was W.M. Supplies, which, in the mid seventies, was in the process of becoming an important supplier of disposables for hospitals, care homes and other care facilities. I had felt in my bones that W.M. would eventually outgrow and outshine its parent company — a judgement that proved correct.

I wouldn't let my instinct about new machinery drop. I insisted that we had performed miracles so far in somehow making the plant pay, but if we stood still then we were finished. The 'discussions' often became so heated that Darrell promised to bring it up with the board.

He returned from a meeting one day to say that he and Edwin had decided to look at new plant in Europe immediately. They departed the next day.

We despatched batches of our raw materials to several machinery manufacturers for testing (including Platt International in Britain), and I waited impatiently for results and decisions. Nothing happened, except that Platt's twice said they had lost their samples, unsurprising from a company whose machinery had never been much use anyway.

We eventually got our new machines from Germany after I constantly nagged over a period of months. The difference in quality and precision was startling. Everyone was impressed with these Ingolstadt open-end spinners and their carding engines. Within two or three years, we had clearly entered the modern age: we were producing quality yarns, and had trebled our production with just over half the original workforce. The workplace changed almost overnight, and ensured survival for at least another 20 years.

I do not have space to write about all the myriad crises that occurred during my 20 years at Park Mill: the move to shift working; the lost orders due to customer problems; the painful redundancies; the part-ownership of a successful business and then its relinquishment when we disagreed on working practices. That would require another book in itself.

Nothing that happened in that mill was ever straightforward or easy, like everything else that I had faced all my working life. William always ventured into territory sensible people would shun!

40

TURNING POINTS

The 1970s saw great changes at work, but it was also a busy time for the Cribb household.

Joan's mother Ivy went into the Royal Oldham Hospital for an operation in October 1970 and never came out. She died on the 27th of that month aged 73, sadly aware that her husband Ernest had indicated his repugnance at having his wife return home wearing a 'bag'. She would not have survived anyway, but maximising her unhappiness was unhelpful and it upset us so much. She was a quiet, gentle soul and had always been a friend, easy to get along with, loved by Joan, but unfortunately dominated by Ernest.

83 Birch Avenue had provided a precious family home. The five of us became accustomed to sitting around the dining table together and sharing our lives. Joan and I experimented with cooking; I experimented with wine-making. Over time we acquired a few more possessions although nothing grand. I put shelves up in the living room and the books I had lovingly brought from St Andrew's school, including the Boy's Own Annual, took their place

there. Gradually we added newer books and a few ornaments. The children started to accumulate their own possessions and to shape their own lives. Caroline began making her own clothes; I would come home to find that she had covered the living room floor with pieces of cloth that she had cut out and tacked ready for sewing. Later, when we entered the 'hi-fi' era, Mike crafted a set of speaker cabinets to house the loudspeakers he bought to complete his 'state of the art' kit.

Alan was the least practically inclined. Whereas both Mike and Caroline went out to work from an early age, got experience of the workplace and the 'big bad world' and bolstered their independence, Alan showed no inclination to leave his cocoon. I was and remain proud of them all. They are each very much their own person. A modest house containing five big personalities was bound to lead to frictions sometimes, but we basically got along very well and I can think of very many happy and harmonious occasions. I learned things from them during those early days, and in the many years since I have learned more and more.

By the late 70s all three had progressed successfully through grammar school. The boys went to university and gained degrees in law and philosophy. Caroline later gained her MBA while working in adult education.

Joan and I had for many years visited Auntie Alice and Uncle Theo in Fareham, Hampshire, and stayed at Catisfield Cottage. Calling it a cottage always amused us because it was a huge Georgian house surrounded by acres of land. It later became a B&B. Initially seen by us as an odd, old place run by equally 'unusual' owners, we grew to love both the cottage and its inhabitants, especially Poogie, who owned the house, and the mother and grandmother of the family who ran the establishment. Maintaining the building, which had been previously owned by an admiral, must have been a costly, lifetime commitment for the family. Consequently, it was all saggy, worn and tattered. But the love and feeling engendered by Poogie, daughter Piccy with her husband Huub and their children gradually won us over completely. I particularly remember one New Year's Eve when we all stood outside the back door and sang 'Rule Britannia' as the clock chimed the midnight hour.

On every visit we renewed something for Alice and Theo, such as curtains, carpets, beds and bedding, and always left them with a cupboard full of provisions. They were special, courageous pensioners, uncomplaining, loving and inspirational people who made a huge impact on my life.

Amid all the good times, life sometimes throws the unexpected at you. About this time we got some devastating news: Joan was diagnosed with breast cancer, which resulted in a mastectomy to remove one breast.

She said, 'Do you mind a wife with one missing breast?'

I smiled, 'If you don't mind; it just brings us closer.'

In fact, I was beginning to be concerned about her health more generally, but I said nothing.

During the late 70s we experienced one of the many downward cycles in our industry — indeed, in several others as well. Unfortunately for the success of the factory, the owners of the nearby golf course sold off some of their land for housebuilding. As soon as the new homeowners moved in, they complained about noise from the factory at night, about fumes, dust, the burning of waste and other issues associated with manufacture. The complaints brought extra visits from the factory inspectorate, which meant major (expensive) installations to comply with new requirements.

Problems at home and difficulties at work combined in a stressful mix. Darrell was also having problems because his wife was suffering from a serious but undiagnosed illness. He was unfairly being 'blamed' by his father-in-law for not looking after her properly. The stress of family pressures combined with a business downturn affected him deeply. He in turn was very unfair with me, and though I understood the cause, I found it difficult to swallow simply because he became such a different person. Bypassing me to get things done, he often left me ignorant about what was happening. Roy Fitton would inform me at every stage and pose questions about Darrell's unusual behaviour. Meanwhile, I was doing everything I could to keep the business going.

Roy asked, 'Did you ever mention your night visits to look at developments by competitors?'

I shook my head. 'No, you know I don't talk about what I do for this place.'

This conversation referred to the times Roy helped smuggle me into competitors' factories at night under cover of being a trainee so that I could see how they coped with modern installations. I had been assured that no senior member of staff ever visited their night shifts, so I was unlikely to meet anyone who knew me. This was at a time when other companies were ahead of us by using the latest vortex spinning units. I learned a lot before we actually got those units ourselves.

The only other person in the mill who seemed to understand my approach was the company secretary at head office, even though I never discussed details. He saw that I was the only one at senior staff meetings who kept their reports short and said nothing else, remarking that I talked little but got things done.

On one occasion I told our M.D. that the meetings were a waste of time as I had just read from an old report by mistake and no one had noticed because no one else understood or cared what we did. Oddly, I was quite unconcerned about opening my book at the wrong page, fully aware that I could have said almost anything, relevant or otherwise.

However, family affairs and health problems at home became paramount as we moved from the late 70s into the early 80s, so thorny issues at work blurred and became of secondary importance.

41

ALPHA AND OMEGA

Some people learn many foreign languages, acquire degrees and doctorates, become high-flyers or successful entrepreneurs. But how many, I wonder, have real wisdom, that indefinable, rare, elusive and precious quality I found in Joan. Academically, she had struggled to obtain her Membership of the Society of Chiropodists (MChS) in Glasgow in 1947, but oh, what a wise person she proved to be, and how fortunate we were to have her as wife, mother, friend and mainstay of our family.

That quality spilled over into our children, who have grown up with the same thoughtful, caring attitude that has made life worthwhile and sustained me all these years.

I have already mentioned how Mike fought to regain his health after contracting brucellosis and the great determination he showed for several years to achieve his aims. Alan also needed courage during his early years at Southampton when his sight began deteriorating rapidly as he suffered blinding headaches. After learning that his spectacle lenses changed three times in quick succession, I phoned the eye hospital (more than once) and begged them to look more closely for the cause of such rapid deterioration. I stressed to them that as a father I was pleading his case because he might suffer silently without complaint until it was too late. I never told Alan I had phoned; he may not have welcomed the interference.

The medics responded with the darkroom test, and on hearing about their discovery of pigmentary glaucoma, Joan and I lost a lot of sleep, often holding each other tearfully till we dropped off with exhaustion. The eye condition is very serious, and in those days when so little was known about how to treat it, we were understandably terrified that he would quickly lose his sight. We felt helpless. The prescribed eye drops, apart from making his eyes burn, brought on loss of vision for prolonged periods. This often made it impossible for him to read or study, and at best reduced his useful study time to just a few hours a day.

We never knew the full story of how he managed during those trying times, but his relationship with his childhood friend Jacky helped considerably. They had been close ever since meeting at aged 13, and supported each other in different ways throughout their degree studies. Alan had opted for Southampton University because it was near her family home and also easy to get to Bath where Jacky was reading languages. He spent as much time in Bath as he did at Southampton.

They received their degrees in 1978, and both families converged on Bath where Alan and Jacky were married immediately following her award ceremony. The city was thronged with joyful parents and their successful graduate offspring, and their modest wedding celebration at a Forte hotel was a happy one.

I need to mention that being the youngest in the family, Caroline always felt 'left behind' and a bit awed by her brothers' academic abilities, never appreciating that she was also at the front of the queue when brains were given out. Indeed, she was blessed with emotional intelligence and practical wisdom as well as academic ability. I have been lucky to be one of the many beneficiaries of her intelligence and care. Caroline and Robert were married the following year, but before Mike and Judith tied the knot — in 1984 — I had relinquished my job at the mill and started a degree course of my own.

Why did I embark on such a seemingly rash decision as giving up paid employment to go back to school? There was not one isolated reason for my apparently crazy action, but rather a combination of things pushed me in a new direction.

Pressures had been mounting at work, not helped by being made to feel foolish by someone — Darrell —who was under pressure himself. He wasn't thinking straight, and suddenly rejected all my sensible requests, a situation completely without precedent. Even safety requirements by the factory inspector were ignored on grounds of cost. I was subsequently held personally responsible for those refusals by the factory inspectorate who threatened me with sanctions if I did not comply with their requests.

Things came to a head when I was accused of not caring about what happened, an almost laughable accusation of someone who had moved heaven and earth to make the place pay. The straw that tipped the whole balance came with a request that I vacate my office because it was needed for something else (with no explanation of what it was), which showed an uncaring disregard of where I could be relocated. It was a really bizarre situation, which illustrated how very unpredictable a normally sensible and decent person can become when stressed. Finally, and very importantly for me, 20 years at one workplace was as much as I ever wished for. I felt I was being taken for granted like a piece of old furniture.

Underlying this comparative trivia was my real concern for Joan's health. I felt that we needed to be together much more than before, one of those unexplained instincts that often emerged unbidden throughout my life. They were feelings I could not ignore.

During this period, Joan's father Ernest asked me to buy a bungalow for him. He handed me the money in cash. Why he would not do it himself was a question I have never been able to answer. By this time he had also found himself another wife, someone he met on a bus, as it happened. It was clear that he wanted her to take care of him, and she often appealed to us for help when she was unable to cope with his demands. We always obliged willingly, fully aware that she was using us. When he died four years later she did not want any further contact with us. Auntie Alice wrote to her, asking her not to forget Joan. She replied with a solicitor's letter stating that all further communication had to be made through their office. Two days after Ernest's death there was another man living with her in the bungalow. She inherited everything he left. The solicitor handling his affairs was stunned to learn that he had a daughter, having been given the impression that he had no children. Joan said that his inheritance was not important, however great, and had no wish to pursue the matter.

Back at work, I had to choose the right moment to leave my job. When I gave my notice, I was not surprised by the bosses' reactions.

'Please stay, we will double your salary; choose a luxury car; take a few weeks off on full pay; what else would you like?'

All this from my friend Darrell who suddenly emerged from his cloud and became genuinely concerned that he would lose me. He could not accept that I needed a change, and was certain I was going to a better paid job. After all my rejections, he still insisted that I could take my time about making any decision.

When he believed he was losing the battle to persuade me to stay, he said that I would lose all my pension rights under company rules. It seemed odd to me that after 20 years (and all my efforts) this could happen, but I repeated that it made no difference whether I left empty-handed or not. I had always been resistant to the lure of money and very fortunate in never being in a position where it was a matter of life and death.

However, he came back later to announce that the company would operate a 'negotiated redundancy' to allow some recompense for all I had done, a scheme that made me smile when the details emerged. I could leave with the maximum allowed under company rules: an immediate pension of just under £1,000 per annum, a 'very small' lump sum, and I could buy my car at the written-down book price. The one obligation needed to enhance my pension was to live long, as it was designed to increase by 5% annually, so I am trying to fulfil that requirement. As I write, it is just beginning to be recognisable as a real income.

The awkwardness of my leaving should not reflect badly on the wonderful people I was lucky to work alongside. For my leaving do, they managed to smuggle Joan into the far end of the building, then presented me with a pendulum clock, carefully inscribed on the back with their thanks. Joan received a bouquet of flowers. They even asked her if she could persuade me to change my mind and stay on as manager.

I left on 2nd September 1982, and applied for courses at Manchester University, Manchester Polytechnic and the Bolton Institute of Higher Education. For the first two, I would have to wait a year (with a one-year entry course for the first). Bolton phoned me and offered me an immediate interview. Alan advised me to accept the course at their Chadwick Street Campus, a small separate offshoot that only offered three degrees. I was accepted to start without delay. He knew that all I wanted was to refresh my mind, spend more time at home with Joan, and have an easy journey to and from college — door to door took 20 minutes. The faculty boasted several Oxbridge-educated lecturers with doctorates, especially in the philosophy department. Together with the subjects of history and literature, it was exactly what I needed after spending years in the world of profit and loss.

Everyone was required to take history, philosophy and English for the first year, then later drop one subject and finish the course with the other two. Though I loved history, it was the subject I dropped after the first year to focus on Lit/Phil because they were more challenging areas for me. My history lecturers and head of history were amazed at my decision because they assured me I was on track for a first at the end of three years, but my reasons for studying were not quite the same as theirs.

As always, nothing ever progresses the way we would like.

42

'THOUGH MUCH IS TAKEN, MUCH ABIDES'

My study course allowed Joan and I to see more of each other throughout 1983. My time at college was more relaxing than anything I had done for many years, enjoyable even, and offered new perspectives, even though gaining a degree was not vitally important to further my career prospects.

We were so close that it is impossible to know in whose mind unspoken broodings originated, but we both simultaneously began feeling uneasy about our future. Joan expressed her fears by saying that we had too much of everything for it to last, by which she meant our intimacy, the unbelievable depth of our relationship.

She said, 'I worry because anyone who has been given so much cannot keep it forever.'

I knew what she was saying, but we were fortunate to have been given it in the first place. I tried to push negative thoughts away.

BIHE took a high proportion of mature students and I discovered that a few were struggling to keep up. Some dropped out early, either because they were afraid of failure or simply did not like the courses offered, a common problem for mature students right across the higher education system. I enjoyed the open environment, so I was one of the dogged ones who struggled but stayed on. I found one or two others who asked for my help and in so doing helped me focus more than I might have otherwise done.

Many struggled with philosophy, unable to get beyond issues like Is this table real, How would we know and so on, not appreciating that asking these kinds of questions was just a spur to less restricted and more disciplined ways of thinking.

Following a literature tutorial with Dr P, he handed my paper back with the remark, 'You have a problem.'

Baffled, I asked, 'What kind of problem?'

'It is too easy for you because you can get by without much effort.'

Perhaps he was right, but as long as I enjoyed the whole experience did it matter? Much of my effort was employed in helping others get through, which was more satisfying. Although I met plenty of people who wanted to 'better' themselves, there were lots who took a different attitude.

A marked paper was handed back to one student during a literature tutorial, with the gentle remark, 'You ought to read the book again because you have not understood it properly.'

The student said, 'Oh, I never bothered reading it at all; I just used the short notes about it.'

It made me angry the way he treated a decent tutor in such a cavalier fashion. When we met later in the junior common room, I said to him, 'That was unforgivable. You could have remained silent instead of being so rude. You don't deserve a place here.'

'It's all stupid nonsense anyway,' he said. 'I may as well get away from it and not waste my time.'

He was true to his word. He never returned after that day.

Another mature student protested during a discussion about poetry, saying that Bob Dylan wrote better lyrics than anything he could see in the books we were looking at. He also departed. I have read recently that Dylan's songs and lyrics made a profound impact on society and that his genius will be recognised in time, so who am I to argue.

A thirtyish female flamboyantly dressed in bright colours, which I quite liked, reacted fiercely to one of my innocent comments about a character in a novel.

She snarled, 'You middle-class people have no idea what life is like, sitting comfortably in your lofty towers. You need to live in the real world first.'

I was stunned, unable to comment.

Meeting a cross section of people from all walks of life was in itself a sort of education, like the Scottish girl whose mention of her 'red ladder' kept me guessing until I actually saw her red Lada car. We often joked about her heavy Scottish pronunciations and had many laughs about the way she used her words, but she gave as good as she got and we enjoyed the banter.

A crowd would sometimes go to the pub for lunch with the usual talk about pairing off with each other.

One female remarked, 'Leave Bill out of it because he loves his wife and won't play around.'

I wondered if it was written on my forehead.

My age and life experience had many advantages and I was treated by some lecturers as a friend who often asked my advice about whether they sounded boring or otherwise, confiding in me where they may not have opened up with younger students.

I was fortunate in having a very bright girl as a friend, an accidental grouping throwing us together from the start. Geraldine was one of those exceptional students, a talent recognised within the first week by the college, and I heard later from one lecturer that they were certain of a good first degree from her. She fulfilled their prediction.

Most lectures and seminars were between 10 a.m. and 3 p.m. — the shortest 'working day' of my life! Consequently, it left me with plenty of time to enjoy home life and other pursuits. As a speed reader, I could absorb as much as I needed, dash off an essay reasonably quickly and move on to other things, such as taking precious holidays with Joan.

We took short breaks, at Scalby near the east coast, at Ironbridge, and also enjoyed short drives around local beauty spots. Sometimes we took a picnic on our drives, fitting them in between Joan's sessional chiropody work and the odd day when I had no lectures. One short drive would take us to Tandle Hill Park, where we could walk through woods and across open meadows. Joan loved the place. She had earlier stayed as a guest at Ravenna on Tandle Hill

Road, the house once occupied by John Hall, her former employer and friend.

Second-year studies at Bolton began with great hopes for making progress in my Lit/Phil choices. I was also able to help some of the new intake to settle into unfamiliar surroundings. There were more new faces, new challenges and opportunities to do something different — a mix of circumstances that have always refreshed my energies and indulged my joy in meeting new people.

Alas, I had been so successful in deliberately pushing aside my unease about my future with Joan that even on that fateful Sunday in early March 1984 my much vaunted instincts did not register, certainly not soon enough.

Joan woke that morning and said that she had tummy ache, so I suggested a stay in bed with a hot water bottle to ease it. Two hours later it was still there and I became concerned enough to call our GP, despite Joan's protests. Following examination, he said she should go into hospital right away.

Joan said, 'Can it wait until tomorrow?'

He agreed, reluctantly, and left us. Ten minutes later he rang to say that he had changed his mind and that an ambulance was on its way. She was admitted to the Royal Oldham Hospital by mid afternoon, examined by a doctor, and was on the operating table at midnight for surgery on what turned out to be cancer of the colon.

Early the next morning I arrived at the hospital and asked a senior house officer about her condition. I was shocked by his answer. She was not expected to survive much longer than another day. Her cancer was complicated by faecal peritonitis, and the surgeon had been unable to perform a full or clean operation because everything inside was in such a mess.

I found her lying in a bed looking really bad. I knelt down beside her and asked her not to give up, pleading with her to fight for life and heaven knows what else. I refused to accept that my beloved Joan was leaving me. The ward sister led me away gently, but I refused to leave and returned to repeat my entreaties. I began to doubt my sanity, the way I carried on, longing to hear her melodious voice, unwilling to believe that I might never be lifted by it ever again. I was walking a fine line above an ever widening abyss with nothing but blackness below, yet I was determined to somehow cajole my lovely wife back to life.

She had been fitted with a colostomy bag, but it remained empty because nothing was functioning. Sister said that it was vital for her survival that it did, so I asked Joan to use all her willpower to make it work. Was I really so demented at that stage, expecting a response from someone weak and barely alive? I was a desperate man reaching out, begging for a miracle.

When I was finally persuaded to go home by Sister Audrey Valentine, she promised to phone me if there was any change. Later that day she did, tearfully happy that Joan's system was functioning, indicated by deposits in her colostomy bag. Apparently, both Joan and Sister had wept together in relief. I returned immediately to once again kneel by her bed and urge her to keep fighting.

Her recovery, adorned with all the usual drips and tubes, was painfully slow. A couple of weeks later she was moved to a continuation ward at Boundary Park Hospital (now the Royal Oldham). During that week, our son Mike and Judith were married, on 18th March 1984. Joan insisted that their wedding plans should go ahead, and that I would attend for both of us, which I did. After the reception the newlyweds arrived at the hospital, still wearing their wedding finery. The sister asked them to walk through the ward to lift the spirits of the patients before joining us in a small side room reserved for the occasion.

When Joan eventually came home, her spirits were so low that I had great difficulty getting her to eat anything at all. I struggled for a long time, tempting her with minute spoonfuls of liquidised food. She was brave, and responded as well as she could with every unappetising spoonful. Very slowly she began taking more reasonable quantities, enough to bring her back to a state where she looked almost like her former self, even though she remained very weak.

A month later we attended the hospital to check on her progress. I shall never forget when Mr J.S. Duthie and Mr Degianis came out together, completed a circular walk right around us and stared in utter amazement at Joan. They were stunned by how well she looked and both said they could not believe she was the same person they had last seen.

Despite her improvement, they said that she would need one or two more surgical explorations to remove the bits that were initially impossible to locate before they created serious problems. We suspected that her reprieve was temporary, so with a fresh opportunity to live our lives together again, time became even more precious and we were determined to use it. I couldn't bear to be away from Joan during these valuable days so I requested a break in my degree course to care for her.

43

A REMARKABLE LIFE

Despite all the inpatient procedures and blood transfusions, Joan told me that those final 20 months of her life following the first operation were the most revealing and uplifting time she had ever experienced.

I apologised for exhorting her to live on and endure the trauma of those procedures, but she said that in many ways 1984 and 1985 were the most rewarding years, filled with love from family and friends. She admitted how astonished she was at the great esteem in which she was held by all who knew her. She never realised just what an extraordinary woman she was; she never considered herself as anything but ordinary. I had frequently tried to convince her that I was lucky she had chosen me to be her husband, even though that gift had taken time to filter through my conscious mind. Joan said she was lucky to have been granted those final years.

Then we had a welcome visitor. A tall man made even taller by a great mass of hair arrived at our home in April 1984: Keith Town, the Methodist minister from Heaton Park

Church who had conducted Mike and Judith's wedding ceremony. When Joan was able, we attended a few services on Sunday mornings. The minister proved to be friendly, supportive and inspirational.

We also managed a few holidays between Joan's hospital visits, driving to Hampshire to see auntie and uncle in Fareham, and accepting an invitation to a social event at college.

In September 1985, Joan expressed a wish to see the sea, so we returned to Scalby and spent a day at Robin Hood's Bay. She sat in the sun and chatted to a lady on the bench while I walked down towards the shore to watch the seabirds. I remember being given a lesson about the different species of gull by an expert, but all I can recall today is that some turnstones were there. My lovely wife took in the view, the warm sunshine, the sea air, and enjoyed a pleasant chat with that friendly lady. Small pleasures, but important ones.

Her final hospital visit was for yet another blood transfusion in November, when I was told that her cancer had spread to her liver, and that further transfusions would not help. I offered to break the news to Joan myself. The night sister had already moved her from a small room to an outer open ward, telling her that those rooms were reserved for 'really ill patients'. I told Sister Valentine that even though Joan had shrugged it off, it upset me that anyone could be so crass.

There is no diplomatic way to tell anyone that their time is very limited, but somehow I managed it. After the shock news, Joan asked me to take her home, which I did. She occupied the bed in our front bedroom. Once settled, she sat up straight, looked at Tandle Hills through the window on her right, smiled and said, 'Now I'm happy, I'm at home with my favourite view.'

She then lay down and slept soundly.

I slept in the back bedroom to allow her space, but got up often at night to sit with her, and we talked more than ever — going over our lives, recalling happy times, things we had done together. We even sang songs we loved from some of our favourite films such as South Pacific and Funny Girl.

When I said that I would be willing to change places to give her back a life, she smiled. 'I know,' she said, 'but life without you would be meaningless for me.'

The practical and caring Joan asked me, very gently, 'Please go on and live a full life, there is so much more you have to do, and I know you are strong enough to do it. Finish your degree; it will give you a purpose, and also be there for our children. They will need you for a long time.'

Suddenly, she laughed, and said, 'A funny thought, I will never need false teeth.'

She reminded me not to forget the family just down the avenue from us who had lost their father, who we always helped every Christmas. After discussing some very intimate details of our own, she came out with a surprise request.

'Keep in touch with Shirley, she should not be on her own.' She paused and, with her wonderful, wickedly impish grin, added, 'And neither should you.'

Shaking my head and returning her smile, I said, 'You persuaded me to marry you in the first place because you were sure it would be good for both of us and now you are trying to organise my future. Always concerned for others!'

She never failed to make me feel warm and happy, even so near to the end.

The Shirley to whom she referred was Mr Duthie's secretary and personal assistant, who had been such a great support beyond the call of duty throughout all Joan's hospital visits, popping in to see her whenever possible. Though I had met her, Joan knew Shirley far better than I did, and I knew she liked her.

Joan's stay at home lasted a week, a sad but rewarding time for both of us and for all the visitors who came during those last few days.

I think it was very early on Thursday morning that she said she wanted to stand up, so I helped her to her feet. She put her arms around me and held me close and very, very tight. I wondered where all that strength came from, especially when it lasted so long, perhaps 20 or 30 seconds, and with such undiminished power that I was actually holding my breath. I felt that she was giving me something special, her love, her blessing, all her strength — and also saying goodbye. I have never forgotten that last benediction. It will always sustain me.

Joan got back into bed, utterly spent, having given me everything she could. She never got up again. From that moment she began fading slowly, drifting into long, deep sleeps then waking for shorter periods. Even though her speech was affected her awareness was not.

I went downstairs and opened the door. Everything outside was white and still, the first snow covering the entire scene like a soft blanket. It was a moment I shall never forget. I quickly wrote a few lines expressing my feelings, never altering a single word. It remains today unchanged.

I had no idea how long my Joan would last, but her sleep became ever deeper through Friday and Saturday, and it was late on Saturday evening, 30th November 1985, when she finally stopped breathing and our world suffered a profound loss. In another nine days she would have been just 60.

Sleep on, my love
I watched you struggle with the gate
And start the long climb upwards,
I saw you hesitate, as though unsure,
You tried to speak, but no word would come.
Behind you, the early risers,
The first car, snow on the ground
And a Christmas card framed in the window.

The Winston Churchill and the Irish yew
With all the other conifers, snow-capped
Still, silent, no breath of wind
A Christmas scene in November
Just for you, my love.
Christ came for you, and now he beckons
From the distant peak.

The night is fading, but sleep on
For you are seeing a new dawn
Brighter even than the white snow light
A brightness reserved for those like you,
The gentle and unselfish souls
Who lived and gave their all for others
Those fortunate few who had your love
And time, and tenderness, and wisdom.

These last two years were hard and filled with pain
But yet had sweet moments of bliss
When together we loved and laughed
And remembered those times
Those times when we were young
And strong.

W.J.E. Cribb
November 1985
For Joannie

44

KEEPING MY PROMISES

Our children have always been considerate. That night, Alan and Jacky went home, returned with a few things and said they would sleep on the bed settee. They refused to let me be alone at night during the following week because they were concerned by my state of mind. Perhaps they were right. With access to her strong sleeping tablets and the rest of the Brompton Cocktail we had been administering to Joan, I might easily have decided to follow her into oblivion. I felt that my life had drained away. However, remembering my promise to Joan, I realised that the loss of one parent was more than enough to bear for the family.

Mike organised the service at Heaton Park to celebrate her life, and shared the service duties with Keith, both showing great courage and control when talking about her. It cannot have been easy for him, and we were all grateful for his part in it and the way he spoke about his incredible mother.

Joan was cremated at Blackley Crematorium, Victoria Avenue, Manchester 9, and her death recorded in The Book of Memory on the page for 30th November 1985, along with my words below her name.

Cribb, Joan Ashton.

Gentle, wise and kind, her love was joy, sustaining, warm,
Her life inspired, is inspiration now.

The next few months became blurred in my memory and I could hardly remember what I did each day. When I noticed people I knew attempting to avoid me by crossing the road, I would say, 'Please don't, and please keep on talking about Joan even if it makes me cry, I need it to stay sane. Please help me.'

While cutting the hedge in front of the house one morning, an elderly woman stopped to say hello. She enquired gently how I was coping with my loss. She was a stranger to me, so I asked where she lived. It was nearly two miles away going towards Middleton, but seeing the query on my face, she said, 'Everyone for miles around knew how very close you were and we all feel your loss deeply. Our thoughts will always be with you'.

Those words helped me more than she could ever know. I cannot remember seeing her again.

I wrote down my feelings over and over again, tearing up the sheets of paper every time, pages often wet with tears. Perhaps it helped a bit; it may have afforded some kind of release. There were so many cards and letters of condolence that I lost track. Eventually I filled two plastic bags hoping to deal with all of them later. I can't remember whether I managed to do so. It is all a huge blank.

One visitor was a friend from Park Mill who attempted to divert my attention by telling me that the company had made a loss (after 18 years of profitability) in the first full financial year after my departure. Apparently, no one could understand why.

He said, 'Really, do they need to ask?'

Where the building once stood, there is now a large housing estate. A stranger would never know that it had ever existed. All the other mills in the group had suffered the same fate several years before.

Now, approaching the 30th anniversary of Joan's death, I can still recall her serenity, its beneficial and lasting effect on all who knew her and were inspired by that ordinary yet extraordinary, special human being.

In trying to honour her memory, I have attempted to remain true to my promises to Joan. I have seen my children grow and develop as a credit to us. I have remarried (Shirley, naturally) with whom I have done so many new things. We often talk about the Joan we both knew, loved and admired.

Our three offspring and four grandchildren have welcomed Shirley into our family circle, treating her with the same love and respect they would have given Joan, and I am so grateful for that. They insisted that I should do the same.

With their help and guidance we have travelled to many places such as France, Spain, Italy, the Canary Islands, Channel Islands, the Balearics, Czech Republic, Scandinavia and even, at the turn of the century, to Delhi, Agra and Jaipur, India's Golden Triangle. We even managed a visit to my old school in the foothills of the Himalayas. As Alan later commented, the journey was to 'wrestle with monsters', words from a short poem he dashed off for my 70th birthday.

Since Joan's death, I successfully completed my degree, worked for a quango, been involved twice with start-up companies, helped to maintain the flow of talking books in the Oldham area, took up martial arts for two and a half years, moved house twice, joined a voluntary organisation and a men's forum (becoming president for one year), helped a friend write her own life story, started Nordic walking and began going to a gymnasium regularly.

Filling in the details from the last four paragraphs would fill another book of memories. It was never my intention to go beyond 1985 on this occasion, but have much more to do if time and health will allow.

45

FIVE RIVERS

Early this morning, Saturday 12th September 2015, I looked at the Ribble Estuary through the window beside my desk. When the trees partially obscuring my view begin shedding their leaves, soon that view will become clearer. Thinking about it offers a clue to why I wanted to see again that signpost to 'Klundy' that I mentioned in the opening to this book, even though no other life-changing signposts ever existed for me in any physical form.

Why, in the year 2000, several weeks after attending a July wedding in Lytham St. Annes, did I get a sudden urge to move from Oldham to a town I had seen just once? Now after 15 years it is a place we have grown to love.

I seem to have flowed willingly with the five rivers in my life, from the Irrawaddy in Burma to the Rilli in Kalimpong, the Irk in Oldham (which joins the Irwell near the Salford/ Manchester boundary), and now to live near the Ribble Estuary in Lytham.

Our wide estuary fills and empties with the tides, a river apparently disappearing for spells just like the Irk and

Irwell, which dive below ground in places like the little vale of 'Klundy'. I was intrigued to know that the Irk flowed directly below that sign and the ground on which I once stood, a reminder that many of my earliest memories of life will always remain hidden below ground.

Lightning Source UK Ltd.
Milton Keynes UK
UKOW02f1007021115

261907UK00002B/11/P